Copyright © 2016 by Lani Sharp
All rights reserved. This book or any portion thereof
may not be reproduced or used in any manner whatsoever
without the express written permission of the publisher
except for the use of brief quotations in a book review.

Printed in Australia

First Printing, 2016

ISBN 978-0-9925202-9-8

White Light Publishing House
6 Lincoln Way
Melton West, VIC, Australia 3337

www.whitelightpublishingau.com

❧ DEDICATIONS ☙

This book is dedicated to three very special Rams: Amanda, my best and most enduring friend, and her much loved late father Ken (April 1953 - January 2014, tragically), two most inspiring Ariens who have moved my Universe enormously. Thank you both, for your love, friendship, humour, loyalty, faith and for being such a wonderful part of my journey. Every memory is so precious.

Also in loving memory of Owen, an Aries I only knew for a short time but who showed me the meaning of a pure spirit and generosity, and whose flame will burn forever: 'Eternally Young' ~ April 1984 - November 2002 (tragically).

ABOUT THE AUTHOR

☾ ★ ☽

Lani Sharp is a Natural Born Rebel who just also happens to be an Aquarian, who shunned 'conventional' astrology courses to pursue her own path in the wondrous, inspiring and ever-evolving field of cosmic forces and stellar influences. After failing to find a course or tutor that suited her needs, Lani set out on her own starry Magic Carpet adventure across the skies, partly to discover her own 'truths' about this ancient system, but mostly to prove that one can achieve absolutely anything, including and above all, their dream careers (or lifestyle), if they put their hearts and souls into it. A self-taught astrologer who takes the esoteric and spiritual approach to this much-loved popular art, she has been studying and effectively practising astrology since she was eight years old. When she is not writing about, channelling, practising or teaching astrology, she can be found living her dream life alternating somewhere between her home in Australia's stunning Tropical North or her second home in Victoria's beautiful Dandenong Ranges, enjoying tea parties with her highly imaginative Cancerian daughter, Allira, and their gnome and fairy friends, crystal-wishing, day-dreaming, believing in gnomes, pixies, angels, fairies, magic and miracles, honing her magickal * witchcraft skills, Moon-gazing, Sun-worshipping, Venus-channelling, Jupiter-drawing, assisting others to discover, unravel and follow their true spiritual paths ... or of course walking across rainbows!

* Not a mistake. Magick is a Wiccan variation of the word 'magic'.

★

ACKNOWLEDGEMENTS, CREDITS & GRATITUDE BLESSINGS

★

I would love to thank the following people and entities for their amazing contributions, interest, support and faith in me as I wrote the manuscripts for each of the twelve astrological Sun signs. Firstly, the biggest thank you goes to my Mum, Sandra, and my stepdad, Barry, for their unending support, love, advice, daily Skype conversations, acceptance of our geographical distance, and above all, their inner knowing that everything always comes together in the end. Your support of me and my dreams is appreciated beyond words. Secondly, gratitude to my wonderful partner, Travis, for his patience (no mean feat for a Gemini!), for supporting me every step of the way, and for his acceptance of my 'mad scientist' Aquarian mindset by never trying to break down the invisible 'laboratory' walls I built around myself while writing the books. I would also like to extend my enormous gratitude to the following: Allira, my little Cancerian 'crab' daughter, a soul in a billion, who also had to tolerate and operate within the bounds of her nutty professor mother's antics and focus throughout the writing of the books. Thank you to Nicola, my wonderful Facebook friend, for recommending White Light Publishing House, and of course to White Light Publishing House themselves, for pouring their faith and passion into my project from the very beginning - and an even bigger thank you to the wonderful people behind the company for publishing my work, Christie and Jess! Gratitude also goes out to my dear friends, both near and far, who have inspired in me so many ideas through simply being themselves - especially Amanda and Carlie. Amanda, you have always been my 'astrology buddy' and I have always enjoyed - and learned so much through - our discussions on all things astrology and star signs: the good, the bad and the ugly! Having someone like you off which to bounce thoughts and share ideas with, has always been immensely helpful and appreciated. I have saved my final thank you for The Universe, who always delivers to me exactly what I have asked for, without exception. The Universe is my ultimate *higher power*, my guiding light, my powerful driving force, my spiritual helper, my guardian angel, my eternal friend, my inner motivator, my sympathetic listener, my inspirational teacher, and the fulfiller of all my dreams, including this one, having my very first book(s) published, a long-held dream that stretches way back through the years to my days of being a mini dreamer, inquisitor and stargazer. The Universe has always believed in me, but perhaps more importantly, I have always believed in *IT*.

So to all of the above, I wish to say:

Thank you, thank you, thank you!

.

"We were born at a given moment, in a given place, and like vintage years of wine, we have the qualities of the year and of the season in which we are born"

Carl G. Jung

"There was a star danced,
and under that I was born"

William Shakespeare

INSPIRED BY ALL THE SIGNS

Aries imparted courage and boldness
And helped me dance away the pain
Taurus gave me hugs and comfort
And shelter from the rain
Gemini provided me with laughter
And taught me again how to have fun
Cancer nurtured and sustained me
By reflecting back my Sun
Leo reminded me there was joy
From within myself and above
Virgo awakened my healthy glow
By teaching me how to love
Libra gave me gentle hugs
And judged me not for a thing
Scorpio lent me some of his power
And took away the sting
Sagittarius showered me with gifts
Of words so wise and true
As Capricorn led the way up the mountain
My resolve and strength grew
Aquarius gave me the gift of friendship
And carried me as his brother
And Pisces swam with me to the depths
With a compassion like no other.

Special Note

Throughout the text of this book, and indeed the whole Lucky Astrology book series, I have capitalised the first letter of the word 'Universe'. This is because, quite simply, I feel it is a very special title for the higher power that I personally choose to be guided by, and have accordingly highlighted it as such.

You may also notice that I use the words 'he' or 'she', and 'his' or 'her', when referring to your own Sun sign and other zodiac signs, and never 'he or she' or 'his or her' together. The reason for this is for simplicity, for I don't wish the sentences to be too wordy and therefore the messages within them to be lost. As a general rule, I refer to all six 'masculine' zodiac signs as 'he', and all six 'feminine' signs as 'she', and this remains a consistent rule throughout this book and the whole series.

Your Sun sign, Aries, is a masculine sign and will thus be referred to accordingly.

CONTENTS

	Page
ASTROLOGY	15
THE ZODIAC & YOUR PLACE IN THE SUN	24
ARIES THE RAM	31
QUOTES BY ARIENS	37
THE ARIES CONSTELLATION	41
THE ARIES SYMBOL	43
THE RUNDOWN & LESSONS ★	
THE ESSENCE OF ARIES	46
THE THREE DECANS OF ARIES	58
YOUR ELEMENT ★ FIRE	62
YOUR MODE ★ CARDINAL	84
YOUR RULING PLANET ★ MARS	86
YOUR HOUSE IN THE HOROSCOPE ★	
THE FIRST HOUSE	98
YOUR OPPOSITE SIGN ★ LIBRA	103
MAGIC, DRAWING, ATTRACTION, SPELLS,	
RITUALS, WISHING & POWER	111
ASTROLOGY & MAGIC	116
PLANETS ★ DAYS OF THE WEEK	
& THEIR POWERS	122
YOUR NATAL MOON PHASE	126
SPELLS, MAGIC & WISHING WITH MOON PHASES	129
THE MOON ★ WHAT T REPRESENTS IN THE	
HUMAN PSYCHE & NATAL CHART	136
YOUR MOON SIGN	139
YOUR BODY & HEALTH	148
THE CELL SALTS ★ ASTROLOGICAL TONICS	153

	Page
FIRE SIGN ARIES & THE CHOLERIC HUMOUR	156
MONEY ATTRIBUTES	159
COLOURS ★ YOUR LUCKY COLOURS	162
LUCKY CAREER TIPS	173
LUCKY PLACES	177
GEMS & CRYSTALS	178
ARIEN POWER CRYSTALS	190
YOUR LUCKY NUMBERS	204
YOUR LUCKY MAGIC HOURS OR TIME UNITS	214
YOUR LUCKY DAY ★ TUESDAY	219
YOUR LUCKY CHARM / TALISMANS	223
YOUR LUCKY ANIMALS & BIRDS	226
YOUR METALS	238
PLANTS, HERBS, SPICES, TREES, SHRUBS, FLOWERS, SCENTS & INCENSE	242
YOUR FOODS	247
YOUR LUCKY WOOD & CELTIC TREE ★ MAHOGANY & ALDER OR WILLOW	249
THE POWER OF LOVE	255
LUCKY IN LOVE? ARIES COMPATIBILITY	268
YOUR TAROT CARDS	284
LUCKY 13 TIPS	303
HAVE YOU PACKED YOUR MAGICAL BAG FOR THE JOURNEY?	306
A FINAL WORD ★ TAPPING INTO THE MAGIC OF ARIES	307

LUCKY ASTROLOGY

By Lani Sharp

ARIES

Tapping into the Powers of Your Sun Sign for Greater Luck, Happiness, Health, Abundance & Love

"That which is above is like to that which is below, and that which is below is like to that which is above, to accomplish the miracles of one thing ... the Father thereof is the Sun, the mother the Moon."

The Emerald Tablet, Hermes Trismegistus (circa 3000 BC)

★ ASTROLOGY ★

Astrology: "Divination through the correlation of earthly events with celestial patterns"
'Real Magic', I. Bonewits, 1971

A BRIEF HISTORY

Astrology can be defined as the calculation and meaningful interpretation of the positions and motions of the heavenly bodies, and their correlation with human experiences. Its central concept is based upon this interconnectedness or correspondence between the stars and ourselves.

The word astrology is derived from the Greek word astron, meaning 'star' and logos which means 'word'. Astrology, therefore, literally means language of the stars. It is based on the ancient law known as 'As Above, So Below', otherwise known as the Law of the Macrocosm and Microcosm. The Macrocosm is the Universe, symbolised by the sky, the starry dome that we can see from the Earth; the Microcosm is us - humans, and all other life on Earth. 'As Above, So Below' is a well-known and deeply impressing maxim of Hermetic origin, inscribed upon the famed Emerald Tablet among cryptic wording by enigmatic figure, Hermes Trismegistus, around 5,000 years ago. These four powerful words are adopted by astrologers and believers in magic to explain, in very succinct wording, the meaning behind the art and science of celestial influences upon our earthly affairs.

Astrology and many other magical and occult studies, propose that we are not separate from the Universe, we are part of it. The Sun, Moon and planets all follow exact patterns of movement and their motions can be measured precisely by astronomers. The basic idea of astrology is that all individual parts of the Universe, from plants to animals, cooperate with each other and work together in harmony.

Anyone can apply astrological knowledge in their daily lives, but it hasn't always been like that. At one time, astrology was reserved only for Kings and nations, and only the court astrologer/astronomer could cast and interpret horoscopes. Ancient astrology and astronomy used to be one and the same. To be an astrologer, you first had to be able to interpret the stars in some systematic way, and then track the movement of the Moon and the planets against the background of the constellations.

Astrology, the knowledge and language of the cosmos, goes back to the ancient kingdom of Babylonia and was adapted by the Mesopotamians, Greeks, Egyptians and Romans to incorporate their own deities (as indicated in mythology). It is upon a combination of Greek and Egyptian interpretations of astrology that our present knowledge is based.

In the ancient Mesopotamian world, as far back as 800 BC, people lived precariously beneath the open skies. The skies and the stars which filled them, were the real founders of astrology. Today we are aware that the Sun and Moon exert a profound influence upon our Earthly affairs, but for our primitive ancestors, the heavens, the stars and the planets must have been a matter of great and mysterious significance. Early humankind, its senses influenced by natural processes of ebbs, flows, growth, decay and cycles, tended naturally towards a physical explanation of the Universe. At first, the movements of the planets - and all celestial occurrences - were observed as omens affecting the Ruler and his nation; it was only in Egypt in the fifth century AD that the casting of horoscopes for individual people and the calculation of the planetary positions at the time of birth became widespread.

The first astrologers, the Chaldeans, mapped the stars and later passed this knowledge and wisdom on to the ancient Greeks, who, during the third century BC, developed astrology into a science with the use of mathematical aids and instruments to measure planetary movements. The Greeks were the first to cast individual horoscopes. And it was the Greeks who associated the four elements with the signs of the zodiac. The word "zodiac" can be translated from Greek to mean the "circle or path of the animals." The Greeks not only had names for the twelve Solar phases but had symbols for each, and many correspond with the ones we use today.

The Greeks passed on much of their knowledge to the Romans. During the second century BC, Roman astrologers were primarily forecasters who were consulted frequently by rulers of the church and state. By the early third century AD, astrology co-existed with early Christianity. This harmonious co-existence was possible because it was considered that celestial bodies could foretell events, but did not determine the future - indeed, the stars seen by the shepherds at the time of Christ's birth were only predictors of his arrival. After the fourth century AD, Christianity strengthened and the popularity of astrology declined as Christian reluctance to support 'pagan' or 'superstitious' beliefs became more prominent. The Middle Ages saw a revival in astrology, with courses being taught in universities and other educational establishments, and connections were made between the zodiac, alchemy, herbs and medicine. Astrology was once again able to exist alongside the Church, although many remained suspicious of astrologers.

Around the beginning of the fifteenth century, academics of the Renaissance movement examined the past for knowledge, and ancient philosophies, including astrology, flourished; this coincided with arts and science movements developing. The famous prophet and astrologer Nostradamus lived during this period. Leonardo da Vinci depicted aspects of astrology combined with geometry in his art. Writers and poets of the time, including Shakespeare, alluded to zodiacal influences in their work.

During this period, astrology had numerous practical applications. Agricultural calendars were introduced, indicating favourable planting times according to the phases of the Moon; health and illness were linked with movements of celestial bodies; and emotional states and mental health afflictions correlated with the planetary positions.

Eventually, new ways of thinking led to a split between astronomy and astrology, and by the seventeenth century, the realm of science had developed to such a degree that astrology was no longer taken seriously.

The study of the sky above us has been charted for more than 5,000 years. This fact is known because ancient 'horoscopes' imprinted on clay tablets have been unearthed, dating back almost 5,400 years ago. However, no one knows for certain just how, when and where astrology first began, although it is known that it flourished in ancient Chaldea, Mesopotamia, Babylon and Egypt.

Astrology is a science which has spanned many centuries and still remains extraordinarily popular, and its truths have the potential to speak to and *through* all of us. Long before today's interest in it, men of great vision such as Ptolemy, Hippocrates, Plato, Galileo, Jefferson, Franklin, Newton, Columbus and Jung respected its inherent truths, mythology and eternal knowledge. Furthermore, astrology predates many other 'sciences' - for out of it grew religion, medicine and astronomy, not the other way around.

The discipline of astrology is ultimately a study of the interlocking and interrelated forces of the twelve zodiacal forces, or constellations, that grace the heavens, as they pour their energies into the earthly kingdoms below. As these various energies circulate throughout the etheric realm of our Solar system, these zodiacal entities and archetypes imprint their vibrational frequencies and harmonic resonances upon our bodies, minds, souls and spirits.

ASTROLOGY & THE INDIVIDUAL

Since the earliest period of the history of humankind, people studied the starry vaults of the heavens and conceived that their presence, movements and positions endowed planet Earth's inhabitants with Divine influence. There is much evidence that positions and movements of the planets as seen from Earth at the time of a birth are linked to personality characteristics of individuals. Human energy and emotional cycles are governed by the forces and networks of magnetic impulses from all the planets. Of all the heavenly bodies, the Moon's effects and power are the most marked and visible due to its close proximity to Earth. But the Sun, Venus, Mars, Mercury, Jupiter, Saturn, Uranus, Neptune and Pluto exercise their influences just as surely. In fact, scientists are aware that plants and animals are affected by natural cycles which are governed by forces such as fluctuations in barometric pressure, the gravitational field and electricity in the air. These Earthly dynamics are originally triggered by magnetic vibrations from the atmosphere, or outer space, from where the planets send forth their unseen waves. No living organism or mineral on Earth escapes these immense, if unseen, influences.

The geomagnetic field seems to affect life on Earth in certain observed ways, and these influences appear to correlate with planetary positions. It has been suggested that the fluctuations of the Earth's magnetic field are picked up by the nervous system of the in utero infant, which acts like an antenna, and these synchronise the internal biological clocks of the foetus which control the moment of birth. The foetal magnetic antenna therefore, is sensitive enough to sense these planetary vibrations and fields, and through a combination of inherited genetics and the positions of the planets at birth, they are imprinted with certain basic inherited and 'absorbed' personality characteristics.

Carl Jung, the Swiss psychiatrist and psychological theorist, suggested that the inherent disposition of the individual is present at birth, and is reflected in the patterns of his or her natal chart. Further, he theorised that there is a 'priori factor' in all human activities, namely the inborn, preconscious and unconscious individual structure of the psyche. The preconscious psyche, for example that of a newborn baby, is not simply an empty vessel into which practically anything can be poured, but rather it is this preconscious psyche that gives us the free will to become what we are instead of what others or our environment makes us. The child is not merely a receptacle for the psychic life of those around him or her, albeit sensitive and susceptible to the surrounding unconscious forces in childhood; for he/she also brings something of his own to his experience of them.

Further, Dr Harold S. Burr, who was a Professor of Anatomy at the Yale University School of Medicine, and author of *The Nature of Man and the Meaning of Existence* (1962), asserted that there is order in the Universe, unity in the organism and man is endowed with a soul. He stated that a complex magnetic field not only establishes the pattern of the human brain at birth, but continues to regulate and control it through life, and that the human central nervous system is a superb receptor of electro-magnetic energies, indeed the finest in nature. He contended that the electro-dynamic fields of all living things, which may be measured and mapped with standard voltmeters, mould and control each organism's development, health and mood, and named these fields 'fields of life'.

It can therefore be suggested that astrological and planetary influences endow us with the majority of our characteristics at birth, characteristics bestowed upon us according to our Sun sign and other planetary forces. Other parts of the chart are also highly significant and need to be integrated for a 'whole' picture to form, however the Sun sign is an excellent starting point.

The ancients taught that astrology was one of the keys to the many enigmas that plague humans in their unceasing quest to determine what the meaning of life is, and what their role and place in the Universe is - and this quest still persists today. Astrology, which dates back over 5,000 years, is indeed one such key to unlocking the many secrets of the Universe - and ultimately, the individual self.

"KNOW THYSELF"

"Man, know thyself.
All wisdom centres on this."
Carl Jung

Before the temple of the Oracle at Delphi, the ancient Greeks imparted a special piece of advice that was carved onto one of the portals: "Know Thyself." These two powerful words are easy enough to understand, but much more difficult to apply. Throughout life's inner and outer journey, astrology can provide us with an inner navigational system by which we can be guided towards our highest potential, and closer towards the eternal quest of 'knowing thyself'. It provides the hope that this higher spiritual plane exists and that if we can 'read' and therefore be guided by the unique inner blueprint that our individual birth chart has stamped upon us at the moment we take our very first breath, indeed we can reach this higher spiritual plane and realise our innate potential.

Always remember that astrology is not fatalistic. The stars may incline, but they do not compel. Astrology simply provides us with an inner guide, a blueprint, for our journey through life and the finding of our true selves - and what we do with the resulting knowledge is entirely up to us.

Good luck on your journey!

THE ZODIAC & YOUR PLACE IN THE SUN

The zodiac is a circle of 360 degrees, consisting of equal segments of 30 degrees each. These represent the twelve houses of the twelve astrological signs. This zodiac is how the early astrologers imagined the Solar system to be, a perfect circle with the Earth at its centre, around which the Sun, Moon and the planets revolved. Each sign of the zodiac corresponds to one of the twelve segments, following a chronological order and established according to the rhythm of the seasons and cycles of the Sun and the Moon. But the zodiac itself, or the band of constellations which comprise it, has shifted over the millennia, creating division between astronomical and astrological schools of thought. It has been said that due to this shift over time, one who once considered themselves as an Aquarian, is actually a Capricorn, the sign before it, and a Leo is actually a Cancerian, its preceding sign. This is the result of misunderstandings and differences in perspectives, and explanations around it are beyond the scope of this book, but can be researched further should you wish to delve a little deeper.

From the astronomical point of view, it is true that the zodiac to which we refer today is not situated where it 'should' be, but indeed, nothing is fixed under the celestial vault. And so the starting point of the ancient zodiac does not correspond exactly to the one we can observe today. But for the purposes of increasing your power and luck, let's keep things simple and enjoy the ride; after all, astrology - while based upon many scientific theories, mysteries, scepticism, superstitions, facts, measurable patterns, ambiguities, correlations, paradoxes, contradictions, links, stigmatisms and observations that seek to support, refute, prove and disprove this ancient art time and again - is ultimately meant to be *fun* too!

THE SUN

Earth's Luminary ★ *Our Brightest Shining Star*

Our Centre, Core Self, Identity & Inner Guiding Light

"Perfect is what I have said of the work of the Sun."
Hermes Trismegistus, The Emerald Tablet

The Sun is our essence, centre, source, ego strength, power, life force, will, vitality, creative expression, purpose, life's direction, our sense of identity, and who we really *are*. Our brightest star is the core of our individuality, our inner guiding light. The Sun is externalising, and represents totality, infinity, eternity, the striving toward and ultimate reaching of one's personal destiny, and *completion* in all areas. It is the creative energising giver of life and the 'father' of the zodiac. It endows us with our inherent creative potential and personal identity - our urge to *create* and to *be*. The Sun is our core self, conscious purpose, our sense of creating something out of our own being. It is the integrated personality and represents the *present*, our greatest Gift. The Sun rules the heart and is thus symbolically the centre of Self. Indeed, the Sun *is* the heart and the most commanding presence in our birth chart; the luminary Ruler who governs our essential self and wants to be noticed and appreciated, and above all, to *shine*.

★ KEY WORDS ★

Identity, core self, spirit, life force, power, essence, creativity, higher self, the Father, ego, vitality, pride, individuality, leadership, majesty, inner authority, will, expression, willpower, purpose, the journey, the path and the destiny.

THE SUN ★ THE ULTIMATE SOURCE OF LIFE ON EARTH

Throughout the ages, and indeed since life forms began, the electromagnetic waves generated by the Sun have kept planet Earth habitable for humans, animals, plants and minerals. The Sun is, in fact, the only true source of energy on planet Earth. It provides the perfect amount of energy for plants to synthesise all of the products required for growth and reproduction, which is then stored by plants and ingested by humans and animals who, through many complex processes, utilise these various forms of encapsulated Solar energy - and so the cycle continues. Wood, fuel and minerals (crystals included), too, are merely various forms of this encased Sun energy. In fact, all matter is essentially 'frozen' light. Human body cells are bundles of Sun energy; we couldn't conceive or process a single thought without the molecules of Solar-energised oxygen and glucose.

In essence, the Sun supports the growth of all species, including human beings and microscopic life forms, and without it life on Earth would simply not be possible. The mathematical and metaphysical complexity that stands behind a system of organisation and order so infinitely diverse and intricate as planetary life cannot be truly fathomed, but unerringly and miraculously, the Sun instinctively knows what each species, from a tree to a human, intrinsically needs in order to fulfil its evolutionary purpose and cycles.

Ultimately, the electromagnetic waves generated by the Sun come in a variety of lengths, which determine their specific course of action and responsibility. There are gamma rays, x-rays, cosmic rays, various kinds of ultraviolet rays, infrared, short-wave infrared, radio waves, electric waves, and of course the visible light spectrum, consisting of the seven colour rays.

Most of these energy waves are absorbed and used for various processes in the layers of atmosphere that encircle the Earth, and only a small portion of them - the electromagnetic spectrum - reach the surface of our planet. Although the human eye is only able to perceive about one percent of this spectrum, the waves exert a very strong influence upon us. The waves and rays which do affect us so profoundly, allow all life forms to undergo constant cycles of change necessary for growth and renewal. Physically, we can observe this, but on a deeper, more spiritual plane, we can even *feel* it and allow its radiance to permeate our very souls. Such is the might, force and power of that astonishing ball of fire in our sky: the brilliant, ever-shining Sun.

THE SUN ★ WHAT IT REPRESENTS IN THE HUMAN PSYCHE & NATAL CHART

☼

"The Sun is the most powerful of all the stellar bodies. It colours the personality so strongly that an amazingly accurate picture can be given of the individual who was born when it was exercising its power through the known and predicable influences of a certain astrological sign; these electromagnetic vibrations will continue to stamp that person with the characteristics of their Sun sign as they go through life."
Linda Goodman's Sun Signs, Linda Goodman, Pan Books, 1968

The Sun is our essence, our core self, conscious purpose and sense of identity, our creative potential, our spirit, the integrated personality that shines outward from within us. It is concerned with the present. It is our centre, source, power, life force, will, vitality, purpose, life's direction, what and who we *really* are.

The Sun represents our basic urge for self-expression. It is the 'Solar energy cell' in a person's character, the Lord and giver of life, and symbolises the way in which an individual will shine out to the world. Our Sun is our personal identity and aspects to it from other components in the chart show the ease or otherwise of assuredness and confidence with which one will project and express one's individuality. The Sun sign will also show how an individual bounces back from setbacks and disappointments, their resilience and their general outward expression of energy.

The Sun is the archetype of the Father and represents the primary masculine principle in the natal chart. It indicates how we express and experience our masculine side, or animus, our conscious self, how we express ourselves creatively, our personal potential, individuality, self-expression and personal power. It has to do with courage, power, generosity, creativity, vitality, self-confidence, nobility, self-worth, dignity and strength of will. It symbolises authority and purpose, the *ruler*, and its potential is the peak of constructive maturity. It signifies self-sufficiency and abundance, containing enough energy to radiate warmth and give life to everything around it.

The sign in which one's Sun is posited, and its placement in the birth chart, strongly indicates the level and type of vitality available to the personality (the sign), and in which area of life this may be most strongly directed (the house).

The Sun in a natal chart is a powerful symbol because everything is filtered, at a conscious level, through it. It tells us what we need to do to feel fully alive, the type of engine 'driving' us, what we need to do to be authentic and to be fully functioning. Listening to the special message of one's Sun sign can provide one with greater direction, and a more dynamic energy and life purpose.

The symbol for the Sun ☉ depicts a circle with a dot or 'seed' at its centre, from which the core self, power, creativity and the first sparks of life can spring. The circle around this 'seed' represents spirit, symbolising wholeness, eternity and the never-ending flow of energy.

While the Moon, the night sky's luminary, represents the *soul*, the Sun, the day sky's luminary, represents our *spirit*.

There is a reason your Sun sign is otherwise known as your Star Sign - it's because, quite simply, the Sun *is* a star; in fact, it's the largest, brightest, shiniest one in Earth's known visible Universe. This book is about your Sun sign and how you can become much larger, glow with far more brilliance, and shine brighter than you ever dreamed possible. I wish you all the magic in the galaxy for your dreams to come true and your deepest wishes to become reality, through tapping into the amazing power and inherent potential of your Sun sign. So get set for a galactical ride through the lucky stars of your constellation - and may a shooting star cross the path in front of you as you go!

ARIES THE RAM

★ Cardinal Fire, Masculine, Positive, Intuitive ★

"Primal energy expresses itself"

Body & Health
Head, brain, face, blood pressure

How Aries Emanates its Life Force / Energy
Enthusiastically, Impulsively, Assertively, with Initiative

Is concerned with
★ Self-assertion ★ Initiation, New Beginnings ★
★ Action ★ Daring ★ Challenge, Adventure ★
★ Exploration, Pioneering, Discovery ★ Pursuits ★
★ Aggression ★ Conquest ★ Personal Goals ★
★ Personal Control of Everything ★ Originality ★
★ Competition, Being First, Winning ★ Bravery ★
★ Courage ★ Nobility ★ Honesty ★ Openness ★

Spiritual Aries

Your Archetypal Universal Qualities
The Initiator, Pioneer, Warrior

What You Refuse
To accept failure or defeat, to be second best in anything

What You Are an Authority On
Self-confidence, Taking Initiative, Courage, Pioneering

The Main Senses Through Which You Experience Reality
Action, Freedom, Being, Self, Movement

How You Love
Passionately, Enthusiastically, Arduously

Positive Characteristics
★ Leader and Initiator ★ Original ★ Open-hearted ★
★ Energetic ★ Eager ★ Brave ★ Encouraging ★
★ Takes Risks for Others ★ Inspiring ★
★ Helps Others to Achieve Their Dreams ★
★ Will Give Life for the Loved One ★ Bright ★
★ Defends the Vulnerable ★ Enthusiastic ★ Strong ★
★ Continues Even if Others Give Up ★ Brave ★
★ Accepts Challenges ★ Uncomplicated ★
★ Believes the Best of Others ★ Childlike ★
★ Is an Open Book ★ Optimistic ★ Fearless ★

Negative Characteristics
★ Must be the Boss ★
★ Impulsive ★ Impatient ★
★ Poor Judge of Character ★
★ Brash ★ Insensitive ★ Frivolous ★
★ Dislikes Being Told What to Do ★
★ Immature ★ Easily Bored ★
★ Blind to Effect on Others ★
★ Intolerant ★ Doesn't Listen ★

To Bring Out Your Best

Undertake regular physical exercise; eat the odd helping of humble pie; go on activity-oriented holidays; take on a long-term commitment; write an autobiography; teach others self-confidence; take on a leadership role; lead by example; inspire!

Spiritual Goals

To learn the meaning of selfless love. To be more reflective, more aware of your shortcomings. To become more enduring. To develop a greater awareness of others.

ARIES

21 March - 19 April

Cardinal Fire

♈

Ruled by Mars

"I AM"

Gemstones ◊ Bloodstone, Diamond, Aquamarine

★ Adventurous, urgent, energetic, selfish, pioneering, daring, courageous, impatient, enthusiastic, confident, dynamic, egocentric, foolhardy, insensitive, assertive, zealous, fearless, eager, naïve, cheerful, wilful, brash, direct, arduous, innocent, affable, brave, driven, bossy, impulsive, curious, enterprising, dominating, careless, leader, autonomous, bold, temperamental, rash, hearty, interested ★

"Racing is life. Anything before or after is just waiting"
Steve McQueen

ARIES

♈

**Dynamic ✶ Naïve ✶ Bold
Courageous ✶ Leader ✶ Strong
Confident ✶ Adventurous**

Aries is the sign of the Ram, a hard-horned sheep who leads the pack and keeps the rest of the herd in line. Bold, bossy, friendly, fearless, spontaneous, brave, courageous, enthusiastic, ego-driven, self-centred and active are Aries' most notable traits. Being a fabulous Fire sign, your sign burns brightly but you can burn yourself out just as quickly if you lose interest in someone or something, and you are quick to move on to the next conquest if something new presents itself.

Yours is a sign which thrives on adventure and pursues excitement. Impatient and confident, Aries loves to be first at everything and is flattered and easily won over by loads of attention and compliments. The Ram believes his own hype, but in a most innocent and non-malicious way. Novelty is a big thing for the driven Ram's spirit, and he needs plenty of new and novel stimulation to keep his fire and passion burning. Aries is impulsive, adventurous and initiating, without thought nor care for tomorrow, and never pausing long enough to reflect upon yesterday; today is his day!

A dynamic lover, fun-loving, if a little selfish, friend and an independent go-getter, Aries is the first sign and the energetic leader of the zodiac, blazing through life at a speed that can be dizzying but breathtakingly refreshing to all those who are lucky enough to have one in their lives!

KEY CONCEPTS
★ Inspirational to others ★
★ Courageous and bold ★
★ An adventurous crusader ★
★ Foolhardy and a zealot ★
★ Lacks subtlety and tact ★
★ An egotistical show of bravado ★
★ Blindly loyal ★
★ Egocentric and self-interested ★
★ Acts without thinking ★
★ Direct, intuitive, perceptive and decisive ★
★ The greater birther and initiator ★
★ The fearless warrior ★
★ Leads the way and shines the light on the path for others ★

SOME CORRESPONDENCES THAT ARE ASSOCIATED WITH ARIES

Courage, speed, adventure, danger, strength of will, leadership, heat, winning, hot or sharp utensils, activity, pioneering, surgery and surgeons, enthusiasm, impatience, capability, explorers, firemen, insomnia, enterprise, machinery, spicy foods, loyalty, armed forces, headaches, abruptness, aggression, rashness, bluntness, guns, fire, boredom, welders, mechanics, bossiness, innovation, burns and cuts, competition, vitality, hot temper, fevers, initiative, forcefulness, impetuousness, and the fighting spirit. Take your pick and enjoy the ride!

QUOTES BY ARIENS

"The great thing about rock and roll is that someone like me can be a star" - Elton John (25 March 1947)

"You can't imagine what satisfaction can be gotten from throwing a pie into someone's face" - Emma Thompson (15 April 1959)

"Some women choose to follow men, and some women choose to follow their dreams. If you're wondering which way to go, remember that your career will never wake up and tell you that it doesn't love you anymore" - Lady Gaga (28 March 1986)

"A day without laughter is a day wasted" - Charlie Chaplin (16 April 1889)

"A kiss can be a comma, a question mark or an exclamation point" - Mistinguett (5 April 1875)

"To be free is to have achieved your life" - Tennessee Williams (26 March 1911)

"All I ask is the chance to prove that money can't make me happy" - Spike Milligan (16 April 1918)

"To accomplish great things, we must not only act but also dream; not only dream but also believe" - Anatole France (16 April 1844)

"If you don't have any shadows you're not in the light" - Lady Gaga

"When I did 'The Great Escape', I kept thinking, 'If they were making a movie of my life, that's what they'd call it - the great escape'." - Steve McQueen (24 March 1930)

"Life is a tragedy when seen in close-up, but a comedy in long-shot" - Charlie Chaplin

"One man with courage makes a majority" - Andrew Jackson (15 March 1767)

"War is not the answer because only love can conquer hate" - Marvin Gaye (2 April 1939)

"I'm not afraid of dying, I just don't want to be there when it happens" - Spike Milligan

"Gratitude is riches. Complaint is poverty" - Doris Day (3 April 1924)

"I know very little about acting. I'm just an incredibly gifted faker" - Robert Downey Jr. (4 April 1965)

"Simplicity is the ultimate sophistication" - Leonardo da Vinci (15 April 1452)

"Luck is believing you're lucky" - Tennessee Williams

"Astrology is a language. If you understand this language, the sky speaks to you" - Dane Rudhyar (23 March 1895)

"Failure is unimportant. It takes courage to make a fool of yourself" - Charlie Chaplin

"Ultimately we know deeply that the other side of fear is freedom" - Marilyn Ferguson (5 April 1938)

"The greatest deception men suffer is from their own opinions" - Leonardo da Vinci

"I've never met an animal I didn't like, and I can't say the same thing about people" - Doris Day

"An actor is at most a poet and at least an entertainer" - Marlon Brando (3 April 1924)

"To live one's life in terms of the revelatory message symbolically implied in one's birth chart, is to live a life in terms of the 'sacred' character of existence" - Dane Rudhyar

"Laugh, smile, agree, and then do whatever the [expletive] you were gonna do anyway" - Robert Downey Jr.

"Where words fail, music speaks" - Hans Christian Andersen (2 April 1805)

"Man does not need the society at all, it's the society that needs the man" - Andrei Tarkovksy (4 April 1932)

"A diplomat is a man who always remembers a woman's birthday but never remembers her age" - Robert Frost (26 March 1874)

"The only reason I'm in Hollywood is that I don't have the moral courage to refuse the money" - Marlon Brando

"Obstacles cannot crush me. Every obstacle yields to stern resolve. He who is fixed on a star does not change his mind" - Leonardo Da Vinci (15 April 1452)

"Fill your paper with the breathings of your heart" - William Wordsworth (7 April 1770)

"Two roads diverged in the wood and I took the one less travelled and that has made all the difference" - Robert Frost

"Life itself is the most wonderful fairytale" - Hans Christian Andersen

THE ARIES CONSTELLATION

The signs of the zodiac are the twelve symbolic features that ancient people imagined while observing the heavens. They saw shapes, patterns, faces, and natural and supernatural beings in the stars, from which they established, over centuries, a kind of celestial hierarchy and system based upon their observations. Groupings of stars became constellations, and twelve of these constellations make up the zodiac, a Greek word meaning 'circle of animals', that we know today.

Star constellations are not really self-contained groups but are particularly bright stars that give the appearance of being close together and form distinctive patterns. These are the patterns that over the ages have been identified as animals, deities or mythological figures and heroes. The stars are the living past. We receive their light long after it has left the star itself and so they are a good focus for escaping from the parameters of time. Their stellar influence is analogous with the aura, the bio/psychic energy field surrounding humans, animals, plants, crystals and even places. These individual energy systems interact with the energy waves emanated by other people, and even the cosmic rays emitted by planetary bodies, for psychic energies are not limited by time or distance.

The cluster of stars we know as Aries the Ram, is a small and unremarkable constellation,
comprising three primary stars which form the horns of the Ram. To the naked eye, the constellation of

Aries is little more than these three brightest stars. It is found in the autumn sky, nearby the great square of Pegasus, the winged horse. The triangle of stars forming its horns and nose, and its hindquarters, appear to merge with the rear portion of its neighbour Taurus.

WISHING UPON YOUR STAR

The practice of wishing upon a star is familiar to most of us, and is a mystical superstition that is ingrained in many of us from childhood. As a night-time ritual, you can wish upon your own sign's constellation or that of the sign whose energies you wish to call forth; indeed, you can wish upon any constellation you feel an affinity with. If you can't see a particular constellation in your night sky, you can always meditate on it in your mind, or you can use the traditional technique of wishing upon the first star you see, while reciting the popular rhyme: *Star light, star bright, first star I see tonight, I wish I may, I wish I might, have the wish I make this night!* Any one of the three rituals will hold power for your own special wish. Good luck!

THE ARIEN SYMBOL ♈

Astrology uses symbols or 'glyphs' to represent the planets and signs. The glyph is made up of shapes representing the energy and physical matter of which the Universe is composed, and how these shapes are used in each symbol provide hints as to the properties of the sign or planet it represents.

The ancient view was that there were five elements: Fire, Water, Air, Earth and Ether (or Spirit). Ether is invisible energy, while the four tangible elements are known as 'matter'. Ether, as pure energy, cannot be influenced by any of the physical/matter elements, although it surrounds them and indeed fuels them. The Greek philosopher and scientist Aristotle regarded this idea as a circle (Ether/Spirit) with a cross (matter) in the centre. This glyph is used in astrology as a symbol for Earth, and the cycle of life. All the symbols used in astrology represent the relationship between energy and the 'matter' elements.

The image of Aries is that of a Ram, and its symbol resembles a Ram's head, but it could be interpreted in other ways as well. From a physical standpoint, it could represent the eyebrows and nose, two parts of the body under the governance of Aries.

The glyph consists of a vertical line, indicating a directed, upward and outward gushing forth of energy. The vertical line is designated as the line of destiny or intellect and is detached and objective. There are two curved lines sprouting outwards from the top; all curved lines, whether half or complete circles, are considered emotionally driven and responsive.

The Aries glyph suggests a fountain gushing up from some hidden spring (as indeed the entry of the Sun into Aries heralds the beginning of Spring in the northern hemisphere, when the world of nature 'springs' to life). It also represents the shooting forth of plant life and, by extension, the appearance of new forms on every level in response to some hidden creative force. The Ram, the symbol of Aries, unquestioningly assumes the leadership of his flock and dashes in head down (Aries rules the head) when danger threatens. The unbashful Ram and the word rambunctious suggest the forceful assertiveness associated with this sign. The lamb is traditionally the animal of sacrifice but the entry of the Sun into the first degree of Aries, when the sign is still young, symbolises the sacrifice of Spirit as it descends into incarnation (from its preceding sign Pisces), into the form of matter.

THE AGE OF ARIES ★ 2000 BC - 0 AD

The Age of Aries ruled over the first period of human history that resembled modern-day society. The two millennia governed by Aries demonstrate the traits typical of this sign: extroversion and a love of adventure, both of which combine to create a leaning toward confrontation. Dominated by the rise and expansion of the Greek and Roman civilisations, this was a period of human history during which military might and physical prowess exerted an extremely important role. Roman legions expanded over and ruled much of the known world. The Olympic Games, gladiator contests and other arena- and spectator-based entertainment and sports, started appearing. The age of democracy arose, with the first democratic government being developed by the Ancient Greeks, and Aries' direct approach to everything was reflected in the straightness of the roads the Romans built across their vast empire. The Age of Aries also saw a move from the god-like Kings of the Egyptian culture, to a more secular form of leadership, reflecting the Arien emphasis on individuality and standing on one's own feet.

THE RUNDOWN & LESSONS
SOME QUIRKS, ODDITIES, UNIQUE
CHARACTERISTICS & IDIOSYNCRASIES OF ARIES

"The Ram having passed the Sea serenely shines
And leads the Year, the Prince of all the Signs."
Manilius

"A realist, yet a decided idealist, Aries often defies
emotional description. No one can show such tough,
forceful behaviour. Yet, few others are capable of
such sentimentality, wistful innocence and belief in
miracles."
Linda Goodman

There are two types of thinkers: what I like to call 'right-brainers' and 'left-brainers'. The left hemisphere of the human brain deals with things such as control of speech, verbal functions, reason, logic, mathematics, linear concepts, details, sequences, the intellect and analysis; the right hemisphere is concerned with spatial, music, holistic, artistic concepts, as well as simultaneity and intuition. You could go on to say that the left brain is masculine or yang in quality, and the right brain is feminine or yin in quality. Based upon these very simplistic outlines, it can be further stated that Fire sign Aries dwells mainly in the left hemisphere, with a bit of right thrown in for good measure.

Aries is the positive first sign of the zodiac, and typifies the initial thrust of energy into the world, the beginning, the pulsing seed, the body, the power and the impulse; it also signifies initiative, courage, leadership, enterprise, independence, and the pioneering, indomitable and adventurous spirit. In fact, Aries can be likened to a newborn baby - unsubtle, egocentric, demanding and frequently loud. This comparison is not to be taken the wrong way; in the same way an infant is a bundle of raw, unshaped energies, Aries is a sign of pure simplicity who echoes the baby's motto of, "Me first!" You are completely self-centred, which should never be confused with selfishness, but the Ram does consider himself to be at the core of his personal Universe and cannot comprehend the notion that he could possibly be positioned on the outer edges of anyone else's. If he wants something, he will get it - for, like the baby, Aries is concerned with the world only as it relates to himself. But his blinkered innocence somehow softens this inherent selfishness and aggression. You are always in the stage of beginning-to-become. In Aries the Sun is exalted, warming the soil, quickening the seed into growth, the person-that-is-to-be held up as a constant shining goal.

Astrologically, it is said that we grow into our Sun, being mostly Lunar in our very early years, and Aries is a perfect example of the seedling that is to sprout into the Solar self of older years. Somehow though, Aries realises this Sun within himself from birth, and shines as such. What takes the other zodiac signs many years to recognise, the Ram *knows* from very early on - he *is* the centre of the Universe, and his needs *will* be met by others through his commanding, ego-driven presence. Mars's force towards self-realisation is equally evident in your personality.

Aries is the first sign on the zodiacal wheel, and while there is no real beginning or end to a circle, Aries's function is symbolised as the first in the human experience. Emerging from the stars is an important theme in this sign, and encapsulates the enchanting seeing-the-world-with-new-eyes spirit of the Ram. Aries ultimately embodies the search for Self and will constantly put himself to the test, but needs others to uphold him and bring his inspired ideas to fruition. His innate self-centeredness can make him find it very difficult to give up the Self when it's called for, such as in more mature relationships.

Aries is the Fire element in its most energetic stage, having to do with beginnings. Impossible to ignore, you possess an idealistic, assertive character who is driven by a powerfully robust ego. Headstrong and dynamic, you charge through life. Emotionally the Arien is an adolescent, doesn't like being overlooked, is youthful, projects itself into the immediate environment with force, and your purpose is ever-dynamic. The typical Aries character almost always has a fight or flight stance, ready to take on anything within a split second. Most Aries will choose the fight over flight; ruled by Mars, you even love battle for its own sake. You approach life with the eagerness of the child who hasn't yet learned to be careful of the fire. In fact, in you, we find something childlike that is still apparent even in middle and old age. Your zest for adventure never dies, unless you become a burnt-out case, consumed by your inner fires. Indeed, the danger of too much Fire is that you are, more than most, prone to burnout.

The impulsive urge is extremely strong, and although Aries is fantastic at initiating and inspiring an idea, you will begin the cycle but rarely see it through to completion. Aries is the sign of individuality, the pure expression of Self, and there is an uncomplicated quality in the way your sign's energies manifest. Courage comes so naturally to Aries because your purpose is singular; difficulties are to be confronted head-on, destroyed and surmounted, never avoided, granted surrender or given compromise. It is easy for the 'self-ness' of Aries to be expressed as selfishness, a simple reflection of your sign's benignly insensitive and naïve egocentricity. If Aries appears preoccupied with his own problems and interests, others need to realise that it is not the calculated selfishness of the adult but the naïve egocentricity of the child.

The most yang and active of all the Fire signs, Aries' direct expression and exuberance embodies the pure archetypal male as pioneer, protector and warrior. Although socially unsophisticated, you possess admirable confidence and uninhibited impulses, which lend your character its notorious adventurous, assertive and explorative streaks. And though you push ahead with confidence, often ignoring the feelings or needs of others, you are without doubt the warmest and most generous of all the signs. Honestly believing you can do things better than anyone else, you find slower, fumbling types intolerable and are happy to do the job even if it means you have to trample over others to do it.

Your ruling planet Mars signifies action, initiative, boldness, bravery and bravado. This lends Ariens a forceful character, but although somewhat aggressive and pushy, you have great enthusiasm and an enviable personal drive. Your presence is commanding, you make a great leader or mentor, and your desire for physical and sexual pleasure is notoriously strong. Independent in action and thought, you can also intimidate those who are less forward, with your tactless and direct expression and exuberant manner. Often accused of having a terrible temper, your anger flashes quickly and disappears just as speedily, for you have an inability to remain angry for long - and your outburst is usually forgotten before you or the recipient even know what it was about in the first place.

Although not emotional, you are never lacking in passion. Nor are you prone to introspection, reflection or moodiness. You have a childlike naivety which makes you surprisingly vulnerable, but because you tend towards self-centredness, empathy isn't one of your finer attributes. However, if made aware of a situation or adverse condition, you will fight wholeheartedly for a struggling loved one, the underdog or the disadvantaged. And after helping someone through a rough patch, Aries will always walk the extra mile just to make sure. Your generous spirit often takes you beyond the call of duty and you enjoy doing favours for others. Blessed with the blind zeal of a born crusader, you would give anyone your last dollar or the shirt off your own back, and your example often impels others to do the same.

Spontaneous and assertive, and the most volatile of the Fire signs, you have a childlike enthusiasm for life and your impetuous courage can inspire others to follow your lead. The Aries intellect, although the sign itself is not ordinarily known as an exceptionally mental sign, is purposeful and volatile, but ultimately directed towards the Self, and most pursuits are only undertaken if they serve the Self in some way.

You have the enviable ability to give your full attention to the moment. Impulsive rather than rational, you have a tendency towards snap decisions, which although always astute, are rarely thought out properly beforehand. With your agile, restless mind, details tend to fall by the wayside; you have far more important things to concern yourself with. In fact, you are the epitome of the expression, "Act first, think later." Trouble is, you rarely engage in the latter.

Aries can make the most wonderful of friends, having the refreshing attitude of a newborn babe, in all your innocence, simplicity, purity and all-round heart-in-the-right-place good nature. The Aries character, essentially, is unaffected and unassuming for the most part. Aries feels compelled to assert his individuality, and you will announce your arrival in the world or at a party through any means possible. The full force of his Martian spirit is employed in his battle to *be*, and this is why Aries is always at the beginning of things; everything is perpetually new to his eyes, and it is little wonder that Aries is the archetypal pioneer and explorer. This pioneering and adventuresome aspect of Aries is perfectly expressed in the myth of the Golden Fleece, the tale which the Greeks associated, beyond all others, with Aries.

But while the Ram has a renowned reputation for being a fearless go-getter, he is often still a fragile human being underneath the bravado. Disarmingly naïve, he is fearless with not a trace of cunning; if he is hurt, he will trustingly try again, and any doubts he has are immediately displaced by the next person who is kind to him. An incurable idealist who believes in the best of everyone, he achieves whatever he sets his determination to, and no amount of falls will prevent him from attaining his goal. Aries males, more than any other sign, experience the most difficulty in tapping into and expressing the feminine or *anima* component of their souls, because their focus is primarily on outward achievements and winning the prize, which are not considered typically feminine ambitions. The Arien female, too, can encounter trouble in honouring her feminine nature and can become warlike in her quests rather than succumbing to her undeniable vulnerability and smouldering femininity. But it is still there - in both genders, because it always comes back to the infant child who craves and indeed, needs, nurturing and attention from others for his very survival.

Aries is about the emergence and assertion of the individual ego, and that often includes doing battle with anyone who obstructs the attainment of any goal or object of desire. It is a rare Ram who will wait around resting on his laurels waiting for success to fall into his lap, for the Aries has little patience for waiting to begin with, but chases anything he wants with a furious passion and 110 percent heart - only to abandon it halfway through if something else catches his eye on the way. In any case, you are always chasing after something or some*one*. It is the Ram who has the most dragons to slay, but how many of these dragons are self-created, is unknown, even to the Ram himself. Many Ariens indeed feel the need to do battle, even when no threat exists, but these fights are normally borne from a desire for drama, excitement, action, adventure and even playfulness. Indeed, there is nothing hidden, secretive, complex or complicated about the Ram, and his mental processes are direct and straightforward. Deceptiveness and deviousness are entirely foreign concepts to the simple and refreshingly honest Aries.

Like the newborn mentioned earlier, you often take it for granted that everyone else will dance attendance upon you and gratify your needs. This lifelong demand for attention springs not from arrogance or even an inflated sense of self-worth, but from a form of unaware forthrightness. As the first in the archetypal human zodiacal experience, you are not the most evolved of specimens. Lacking this self-awareness and often ignoring the needs of others, albeit innocently, you don't understand the concept of waiting your turn or considering other factors, for you see life in terms solely of your own boundaries, needs, impulses, wants and requirements, and you quite naturally expect these to be met first.

Fresh and direct, you are completely guileless. Functioning on refreshingly simple levels, to you, black is black, white is white, spades are spades, and daisies are daisies, and you feel genuinely bewildered and even a little disheartened when you find out that the rest of the world doesn't see things in quite the same way. In any case, the complexities of others will at best amuse you and at worst confuse you. Why can't people just say what's on their mind, you despair. But quicker than a camera flash, you're onto the next pasture to call a blade of grass a blade of grass. You have no time for delving too deeply and long-winded debates about the whys and wherefores of everything; quite simply, you enjoy just *be*ing and *do*ing, rather than analysing. After all, a rose is a rose, and to stop and smell it would take up too much of your precious time! Stopping to smell the flowers is not your thing to begin with, but to reflect on it would be even more pointless.

An exceedingly assertive sign who is motivated by 'Number One' and Fired up by Mars, problems are always faced head-on with a view to finding innovative solutions, but you may lack perseverance - and you want everything *now*. Projects and people may be abandoned halfway through, but with a flutter of your sweet eyelashes you are normally forgiven for this. A go-getter by nature, you always know where you're headed, but often ride rough-shod over others in your urge to get there. You are perpetually in a hurry, and rarely stop to think out your plan before you set out on your journey; patience is not one of your virtues. Neither is being a team player. And to you, it's not about how you played the game, it's about whether you win or lose. Winning is your aim every single time, and you have a strongly competitive streak which sees you pit your wits against even the toughest opponent - against whom you more often than not win.

There isn't a malicious bone in the Ram's body; when you offend you do so unwittingly. And although you are quick to anger, you are even quicker to forget; you harbour neither spite nor grudges. Life is far too short! Fiercely loyal, you will defend your loved ones - and your convictions and principles - to the death, and you are unflinchingly courageous, completely unperturbed to stand alone and fight in the face of unilateral opposition. You will rarely compromise your ideals for the sake of courting popularity and your actions are always above board, transparent and clear-cut. Engaging in dubious or secretive behaviours is definitely not your style, for you are unwaveringly honest and expect the same courtesies to be extended to you.

You are rarely defeated in spirit and will fight for something or someone you believe in with all your might. But your burning desire, above all other considerations and aspirations, is to be special. Whilst your Cardinal counterpart Capricorn strives to reach the top, you are only interested in getting to the front. With your tough stance and defiance in the face of the most daunting opposition, you frequently achieve this feat. Whatever life throws at you, you catch with both hands - and never drop the ball. With your indomitable enthusiasm, you can either treat life as a joyful dance or as a competitive battleground - whichever path you take, the choice is always yours - and you always make it with typical aplomb. Perhaps Alan Oken sums up the Aries spirit perfectly in this succinct statement: "Aries is a separate ray of sunshine from the body of the Sun." That he is.

LESSONS TO BE LEARNED FOR GREATER POWER, ENLIGHTENMENT & LUCK

Arien problems and ultimate undoings arise through selfishness, egocentricity, childish behaviour, lack of perseverance, excessive risk-taking, always desiring to be first, and wanting everything *yesterday*. An inherent failure to recognise and accommodate for the needs of others, and insensitivity to others' feelings, creates life challenges for the dynamic and forceful Ram. You need to learn how to lead without being bossy, lose without sulking, and become self-aware by being true to yourself without self-absorption. Reflection, solitude and occasional peaceful surroundings, might also help to draw your softer side out and endear you more to those you love.

The Arien's extreme individualism can be both your greatest strength and your greatest weakness. The Aries sense of 'I Am' and 'I must win at all costs', can lead you to courageous, bold, direct, clear-headed action where other signs may falter; you attack all goals and obstacles head-on and with a determination unmatched by anyone. Never pretentious or engaging in manoeuvres, manipulation or complicated strategies, you possess an enormous and enviable integrity and an energy and single-minded vision, making you a strong force who is usually successful. But it can also bring you loneliness, isolation, enemies, burnout and unhappiness. You might be so determined and headstrong that you fail to notice the reactions of other people - in essence, what is best for the rest of the herd. While words like selfish and egocentric appear not to faze you, the vulnerable lamb inside the Ram is actually crushed when people don't like them. Broadening your goals and learning the subtle art of empathy in your dealings with others will lead to greater happiness and fulfilment for the Arien spirit - and that tender little lamb inside.

THE THREE DECANS OF ARIES

Decans are thirty-six groups of stars that rise in a particular order on the horizon throughout each Earth rotation. These decans were developed in Egypt thousands of years ago. The rising of each decan marked the beginning of a new 'decanal hour' of the night for these ancient people, and eventually three decans were assigned to each zodiac sign. Each decan covers ten degrees of the zodiac wheel, and is ruled by different planetary rulers that rule over the other two signs of the same element (and a traditional ruler, when only seven of the planetary bodies were known). Decans continued to be used throughout the Ages, in astrology and in magic, but many modern astrologers, for whatever reasons, tend to disregard them. Following are brief descriptions for each decan of Aries. Which one do you belong to? Can you relate to the description and the energies of your decan's ruling planet?

FIRST DECAN ARIES ★ March 21 - 30

Ruler ★ Mars (traditional *) / Mars (modern)

Keyword ★ Dynamic

First Decan Aries's Three Special Tarot Cards
The Emperor, Queen of Wands & Two of Wands

Birthdays in this decan range from 21st March to 30th March. This is the Aries decan, ruled by Mars

*. Ariens born during this decan are incredibly dynamic and ambitious, and you possess outspoken, impulsive and headstrong tendencies. Yours is a character driven by ardour, impulses, passions and self-serving motives. With a double Mars influence, you are likely to be a fearless pioneer in your chosen field, as well as being adventurous, dominant, proactive and taking great initiative to get what you want out of life. As a result, your ambitions and dreams are almost always realised - and you never fail to reach the finish line first!

SECOND DECAN ARIES ★ March 31 - April 9

Ruler ★ Sun (traditional *) / Sun (modern)

Keyword ★ Charisma

Second Decan Aries's Three Special Tarot Cards
The Emperor, Queen of Wands & Three of Wands

Birthdays in this decan range from 31st March to 9th April. This is the Leo decan, ruled by the Sun. Ariens born during this decan are powerful, with a strong sense of ethics and morality. Ambitious, motivated and equipped with great leadership skills, you are driven by the force of the Sun, generating radiance, vitality, enthusiasm and influence wherever you go! You have a need to assert yourself and your power, so although you may have an air of charisma, charm and personal magnetism, you may also be perceived as bossy and commanding. Possessing both constructive and creative abilities, this is a most fortunate influence, and you are a high-achiever who loves to make an impact. Generous to a fault and deeply inspiring to others, you like to be the centre of attention, the focus of admiration, the recipient of respect, and the object of desire, but any boastfulness will need to be curbed - because sometimes your Sun's light can be a little *too* bright, burning those around you.

THIRD DECAN ARIES ★ April 10 - 19

Ruler ★ Venus (traditional *) / Jupiter (modern)

Keyword ★ Passion

Third Decan Aries's Three Special Tarot Cards
The Emperor, King of Pentacles & Four of Wands

Birthdays in this decan range from 10th April to 19th April. This is the Sagittarius decan, ruled by Venus * and Jupiter. Ariens born during this period are excellent self-promoters, demonstrative, and attracted towards philosophical and religious quests for knowledge. Love and carnal pleasures may be a predominant feature in your life, but you do adhere to a strict moral and ethical code and have a need for personal freedom. You are sometimes torn between romance and your need to be free from commitments and restrictions, but usually manage to find a happy medium if your lover understands your soul's lofty aspirations. Idealistic, intuitive and generous, you love the company of others, especially when discussions of ideas and the exchange of knowledge are involved.

You strive to learn, you possess a keen thirst for new horizons and adventures. However, your over-idealism and unrealistic expectations may trip you up at times, as you tend to live with one part of your mind always in the clouds.

The decan's traditional ruler based on the Chaldean order of the planets

YOUR ELEMENT ★ FIRE

According to the *Oxford English Dictionary*, the word *element* has a mysterious origin, and was first found in Greek texts meaning 'complex whole' or 'a single unit made up of many parts'. From the ancient up to medieval times, there were only four elements - Earth, Air, Fire and Water - and the occult-oriented also believed in a fifth: Spirit, or Ether. (Cornelius Agrippa called Spirit the 'quintessence'.

Alchemy is a tradition of visions and dreams, and images can combine on different levels of reality. Alchemists have long used images in their illustrations to express the enigma and mystery of their art, and to include all dimensions of our experience. The traditional worlds of Earth, Water, Fire and Air symbolise these dimensions very well. Broadly speaking, and in human terms, Earth corresponds to the level of the body and the senses, Water to the flow of thoughts and feelings, Fire to inspiration and energy, and Air to the world of the higher mind and intellect. Each of these worlds has its own realm of imagery. Aries belongs to the realm of the Fire element.

★ The Passionate Group ★

The path to INSPIRATION

Focused on Identity & Action

Alchemical Associations ★ Transformation, Sulphur and the Colour Red

Key Attributes ★ Energy, passion, decisiveness, illumination, expansion

Symbolism ★ Clear thought, communication, study, connection to the Universals

Governed by ★ The Spirit and Intuition

Fire Characteristics ★ Passionate, energetic, courageous, wild, vibrant, transformational

★ THE MAGIC OF FIRE ★

Fire is the fuel that drives willpower and gives you the energy you need to turn your dreams into reality. Beware, however, as Fire can easily flare out of control. Powerful, dynamic and constantly changing, it is difficult to contain and control, but when used wisely it brings light, warmth and hope to your experience. Without the action Fire drives, you would stay grounded and uninspired - rooted to the spot forever. Fire brings your desires into fruition by bringing determination and bravery - a natural call to action.

★ KEYWORDS ★

Adventurous, energetic, ardent, independent, passionate, enthusiastic, optimistic, impulsive, honest, exuberant, self-motivated, physical, individualistic, assertive, inspirational, courageous, has faith, spirited, warm, takes initiative, confident, extroverted, spontaneous, impatient, restless, simple and direct in approach, creative, idealistic, freedom-seeking, dramatic, forceful, Joi de Vivre! *

* *All these words don't necessarily describe all three Fire signs. Leo, for example, is not necessarily restless or freedom-seeking.*

Fire is fundamentally different to the other three elements, but it is the essential fourth. The other elements are eternal - only Fire has a birth and a death. Fire is ephemeral; even the blazing, glowing ball in the sky, our Sun, will burn out in time. Remember also that you need to nurture and replenish this primal force of expression, as Fire is not self-sustaining and it needs fuel to maintain its heat, light, movement and momentum. Fire is, quite simply, the element of creation, the life force made manifest. The most active and consuming astrological energy, it is the element of spirit, roaming far and wide in search of inspiration and meaning. Fire is also the identity principle. It animates, transmutes and energises.

Fire is associated with the intuitive function and its motivating force is inspiration. Characterised by movement, force and energy, it offers new possibilities, regeneration and a buoyant, spontaneous expression. Fire's essential characteristic is the energetic exploration of life: to conquer, to lead and to travel - both mentally and physically. Fire signs are creative and perceptive, experiencing life through intuition and spirit. Fire is a conceptual and visionary element, ever searching for meaning. Its energy can light up the world, or scorch it out of existence.

Stimulating and spontaneous, it has a warm, passionate, enthusiastic and active approach to life. Fire initiates and motivates, and it is optimistic and explorative. Fire is also connected with heroism, a sense of beginning, regrowth and the future. Aries represents personal development, Leo represents interpersonal development, and Sagittarius represents transpersonal development. They are masculine polarity, extroverted in action.

Fire is strength, power, protection, and the ability to change from one state to another. It is enlightenment and extremely potent but, like Air, it can represent truth and knowledge through purification. The alchemical symbol for Fire is an upright triangle, a male symbol meaning action and movement. Pointing upwards, it represents the path to higher truths, light and transformation through self-motivated activity. But like any magical Elemental energy, Fire has two sides: creation and destruction. It can destroy things for the better, such as the symbolic 'burning away' of old thought patterns, bad habits, negativity, and things we no longer need in our lives.

The Fire element is spiritual, progressive, transcending, visionary, confident, 'birthing', associated with starting points, and a sense of the Divine, is reactive, has faith, philosophical, quests for purpose, is playful, joyful, connected to the 'inner child', ascending, optimistic, combative, has a strong expression of emotions, is straightforward, direct, spontaneous, risk-taking, passionate, forceful, dynamic, bold, humorous, idealistic, and intuitive in the perceiving sense, not the feeling sense.

As the element suggests, Fire signs are a great source of warmth, intensity and light, but they can also be volatile. Exuberant, passionate and motivated, Fire signs are the active people of the zodiac, preferring to lead and take initiative rather than wait for things to happen. Blessed with confident, fun-loving and dynamic personalities, they have a natural flair for boosting talent, morale and confidence, and are usually the driving force behind relationship and family decisions. Fire signs are the extroverts of the zodiac, being charismatic, enthusiastic and assertive, usually being the first to make an introduction, explore wider horizons or conquer new ground. While their natural positivity and optimism can be infectious, they may also be inadvertently selfish, overbearing, bossy and over-zealous in their approach. The passionate Fire signs also like stimulation and drama, and in the absence of excitement, may wander elsewhere to find it. Being impulsive, they may take risks and be compelled to act and speak without thinking, coming across as reckless, careless and tactless. Although honest and direct, they may have a tendency to be blunt. Charming but impatient and impetuous, Fire signs have an admirable lust for life, immense bravery, enormous generosity of spirit, and a fierce and protective loyalty towards their loved ones.

"To be alive is to be burning," asserted psychoanalyst Norman O. Brown. Too much burning, however, can lead to burnout. Too much unrestrained Fire can burn others. When Fire people are out of control, fire extinguishers (water) and stamping it out with a heavy material (Earth) can work wonders. Fire generated by a spark can spread as a forest fire spreads, creating excessive heat and smoke, which can sear and smother.

However, the inner heat that Fire provides is the sustaining life force that contributes to self-confidence, radiance, eagerness, faith, forward movement and healthy creative and sexual expressions. Psychologically, Fire is naturally in motion, catalysing inner light, spirituality and vision. Being an inspirational element, it rises upwards and moves forward, and requires space to expand. Its positive expressions are warming, brightening, uplifting and motivating.

> "Suddenly, the whole orchard was ablaze with light, as if the Sun had risen at midnight. It was the Firebird. The Firebird had come, with wings that shone like gold and eyes that gleamed like crystal … (The feather the Firebird left behind) was so glorious that the king immediately forgot about his orchard. The feather was full of brilliance, like a thousand candles all alight at once."
>
> **Edited extract from Prince Ivan and the Firebird**

As illustrated in the passage above, the fiery spark that sets the process of creation going is personified in a number of mythological fiery creatures. The salamander living in the flames in our emblem is one such. Many of them are birds, like the legendary Phoenix, the mighty bird of Fire which arises from the ashes. There is also the Simurgh, bird of Divine Light in Asian mythology, and the Sun-bird of ancient Lycia, which takes souls and flies them up to the sky after death.

The Firebird, a miraculous animal from Russian folklore, as the previous extract outlines, is the bird of inspiration. It has been said its feathers shine as if made from silver and gold and its eyes sparkle like crystals. It sits upon a golden perch and, at midnight, illuminates gardens and fields as brightly as a thousand lights. When the Firebird sings, pearls fall from its break and the sound has the power to heal the sick. It feeds on golden apples which have the power to endow immortality and beauty to those who eat them. A single feather from its tail will light a room; and one feather from her tail is said to be enough to set you off on a Quest. Fire can indeed set us ablaze with enthusiasm. Sometimes it must be seized with both hands, and once the Fire is ignited, it demands action, energy and risk-taking. Fire is not just for the chosen few, for we all have a chance to find a spark and use it; but once discovered, it demands decisive commitment.

According to the I Ching, the hexagram li/li, fire over fire, suggests that, "A luminous thing giving out light must have within itself something that perseveres; otherwise it will burn itself out."

Fire is crucial to alchemy, because heat is a key agent in transformation. Fire also effects colour changes, another critical component of the alchemical process. Further, most of us have some significant memory, fascination, fear, wonder, nervousness or curiosity about fire. Fire can quickly get out of control, and as such careful regulation of it is crucial, both literally and metaphorically in terms of our own enthusiasm. It can destroy, but for all its destruction, it can provide the perfect conditions for the seeds of new life to spring forth. Fire must be controlled however, for enthusiasm is a useful tool but a terrible master, as it drives out discernment and discrimination.

Red, yellow and orange are the colours associated with Fire, and other associations include the Sun, candles, lanterns, swords, warfare, wands, volcanoes, beacons, torches, salamanders, rams, lions, dragons and phoenixes.

Fire comes from the Sun, our great 'Father' in the sky whose warmth and radiance uplifts us all. As followers upon a magical path, we must possess a Fire within us too - a Fire of vision which brings in its wake strong and true wisdom. For when we are carriers of this flame, we can go forth into the world as a beacon of warmth and light.

Positive Fire Qualities ★ Warm, enthusiastic, spirited, idealistic, honest, exuberant, playful, self-motivated, sincere, action-orientated, self-expressive, open, generous, romantic, illuminating, direct, freedom-seeking, optimistic, future-orientated, self-confident, passionate, creative, individualistic, spontaneous, adventurous, pioneering, initiating, inspiring, spiritual, visionary. Fiery temperaments are positive and extroverted, pushing ahead through life with charisma, confidence and buoyancy. They are demonstrative, dramatic, intense and affectionate, with a strong intuitive quality.

Negative Fire Qualities ★ Self-centred, impatient, unrestrained, without boundaries, pushy, careless, reckless, overconfident, insensitive, wilful, self-deluding, volatile, childish, unable or unwilling to reflect, sulky, lacking in perspective, hasty, angry, impractical, thoughtless, forceful, intrusive, restless, immature, driven by desires and sexual urges, egocentric, extravagant, overbearing, melodramatic, imposing, tactless, comes on too strong, temperamental, ungrounded, wild, hyperactive, impulsive, unstable, inconsistent, clumsy, out of touch with own body, and explosive. Fiery temperaments can suffer from 'burnout' through their excessive enthusiasm, energy and impulsivity, and may feel flat or depressed when life deals them a blow.

THE ARCHANGEL OF FIRE ★ MICHAEL

An archangel is an angel of greater than ordinary rank. They possess a stronger, more powerful essence than the guardian angels, through overseeing and guiding the other angels who are said to be with us here on Earth. The word 'angel' derives from the Greek word *angelos* meaning 'messenger'. To humans, angels are often seen as bringers as all sorts of messages. Angels in all their forms are believed to bring the message of 'spirit' into matter, carrying the blueprints of creation and the Source from the Divine into the manifest world. Angels are not and never have been human; they, like fairies and nature spirits, are part of a different evolutionary pattern – but they do appear to us in human form (usually with wings) because that is what we understand. An angel can be in many different places at once, and with the same intensity and concentration, and wish for us to be aware of them and benefit from them.

There are said to be three categories of angels in the cosmos, each with three subdivisions *. 'Angel' is the generic term and also relates specifically to those closest to the physical. Similarly, archangel may be taken to mean any of the higher orders, and indeed signifies the order just above ordinary 'angel'. Found in a number of religious traditions, the word 'archangel' itself is usually associated with the Abrahamic religions. The word archangel is of Greek origin, and means literally 'chief angel'. All archangels end with the 'el' suffix, 'el' meaning 'in God' and the first part of the name meaning what each individual Angel specialises in. The archangel who rules your sign will be the one with whom you most resonate. The astrological sign is an energy signature, a matrix of a specific stellar pattern that will subtly affect and influence you.

Although there are many associations for the great archangels of the Universe, we must keep in mind there is great overlapping in their duties and guidance. For example, we may say that one is for healing and another for protection, but they can all perform the functions of the others, and each has only areas of greater focus and responsibilities. Four of the multitude of archangelic beings work intimately with the Earth. These are Raphael (Air), Michael (Fire), Gabriel (Water) and Uriel (Earth). Associated with each of these archangels are one of the four elements, specific colours, one of the four directions or quarters of the Earth, three signs of the zodiac, and a variety of other energies and powers. Understanding these associations and considering them in relation to our own paths, can help us determine with which of them we are more likely to resonate. Your sign, being of the Fire element, vibrates to the essence of Michael.

* The first sphere, the *Heavenly Counsellors*, comprises Seraphim, Cherubim and Thrones. The second sphere, the *Heavenly Governors*, comprises Dominions, Virtues and Powers. The third sphere, the *Heavenly Messengers*, comprises Principalities, Archangels and Angels. Of course, all such classifications are a human construct, a way of placing order upon the unknowable and allowing us to perceive something about which we have no words to express. However, as long as we think of angelic hierarchies as a way of working with celestials, of remembering important attributes, and we are able to imagine and experience these beings, this order of angels will prove useful to those wishing to draw upon their messages and assistance.

★ ARCHANGEL MICHAEL'S ASSOCIATIONS ★

Element of Fire
The southern quarter of the Earth
The Autumn season
The colour red
The astrological signs of Aries, Leo and Sagittarius

Michael, meaning "Who is like God or the Divine," is the leader of all the archangels and is in charge of courage, truth, strength and integrity. He protects us physically, emotionally and psychically. Michael helps us to follow our truth without compromising our integrity, and helps us find our true natures so we can be faithful to who we really are. Overall, Michael is the archangel of protection, peace, safety, clarity, balance, and moving forward. This being works to bring patience and a safeguard against any psychic imbalances or dangers. Michael helps us to tear down the old and build the new.

ARIES'S ZODIAC ARCHANGEL ★ JOPHIEL

Additionally, each sign is associated with a particular archangel. Such knowledge can help you to build up a relationship with these beings, based upon your strengths and needs. However, no link is rigid, and as you work with angels you will come to develop your own affinities. When invoking a specific archangel, a useful ritual to draw them closer is to light a candle in that angel's colour, burn some oil or incense of its scent, and hold the appropriate crystal while focusing on what you are needing guidance on.

YOUR ARCHANGEL ★ Jophiel's name means 'beauty of God'. He is the bringer of sunshine, wisdom and joy. He carries the flame of intuition, and his blessings include creativity and inspiration. He is the dispeller of clouds of doubt and thereby increases self-esteem, courage, vitality and strength.

SCENT/OIL ★ Cinnamon

CANDLE COLOUR ★ Gold

CRYSTAL ★ Citrine

THE DEVIC REALMS & FIRE ★ SOUTH: REALM OF THE SALAMANDERS

"Through magick we do conjure the Elements, evoking unto us the special properties of the Life-force for our learning and our coming-into-light. And yet are there secret paths of knowledge that have fallen from the minds of men ... For the way of Magick is a path to sacred knowledge, of reverence and humility - and the world is a wondrous place. Yet how many amongst us have fathomed these depths?"

**Merlin's Book of Magick and Enchantment,
Nevill Drury**

Deva is a Sanskrit word that means 'shining one'. Devas are the life force within nature, and there are four devic realms - Fire, Earth, Air and Water - which contain ethereal elemental spirits or sprites.

Elementals are the building blocks of nature, and close to being true energy and consciousness. The four elements correspond to four different states of matter: energy/transmutation (Fire), gas (Air), liquid (Water) and solid (Earth), which are linked to the four human states of consciousness: inspiration, thought, feeling and practicality. There are four spirits, or elementals, which reside in the devic realms, associated with each element. People have been painting pictures, telling stories and writing about these devic realms for hundreds of years, albeit sometimes through disguised mediums such as fairy tales or children's fantasy stories like Tolkien's *Lord of the Rings*. The power of the natural world is easily observed and since ancient times primal forces have been ascribed to various spirit beings. Belief in nature spirits is of such ancient origin and is Universal; cultures everywhere have names or words to describe them. In the sixteenth century, a famous Swiss physician, alchemist and mystic called Paracelsus * defined these beings as 'Elementals', classifying them according to the element of nature they inhabit. There are four main levels of elemental beings: Gnomes (Earth), Undines (Water), Sylphs (Air), and Salamanders (Fire). The fifth element of Ether is the element from which came forth the other four, and Ether, or Spirit, has never been defined in any particular category, and encompasses the aspects and beings of all the other elements.

Elementals are usually benevolent guardian beings or spirits that look after nature's secrets and treasures in whatever part of the natural realm they occupy. They can only be seen or 'felt' by those possessing heightened psychic abilities, yet they can be summoned by those practising alchemy, spells and magic in order to harness the forces of nature for their own particular intentions. In our modern lives, it may seem as though this magic doesn't exist, but the truth is that most of us are simply less in touch with it than ever before. The consequence of this is that we are destroying vast areas of land, polluting waters, creating toxic landscapes, and disrespecting the laws of nature, which often whisper their messages softly. It is therefore important for us to look at the beauty that surrounds us with true appreciation and genuine regard, and to open ourselves up to the magic resides within it. The four devic realms can teach us much about nature; they act as custodians for the four elements, and learning to work with them is a way of attuning to all the energies and beings of nature.

Elementals are four-dimensional, and have nothing to obstruct their movements. Therefore, they move as easily through matter as we do through air and space. They do require some contact with humans for their own evolution. Helping to direct them is an overseer, traditionally called the King of that element, and an archangel. Each of these elements is affiliated with one of the four directions and each elemental spirit embodies its own special energy. If you wish to re-connect and re-harmonise yourself by working with nature and its messages and lessons, you could begin by learning a little about your element's realm: Your element is Fire, which is connected with the South direction and the realm of the Salamanders.

* Paracelsus is considered the most original medical thinker of the sixteenth century. His belief in supernatural beings, intuition and the invisible causes of illness helped him discover hydrogen and nitrogen. Paracelsus believed that "Elementals are unlike pure spirits for they are mortal, but they are not like man for they have no soul."

★ SALAMANDERS ★

These are not to be confused with the reptile salamanders, although they have the same name. Fire spirits are described as thick, red and dry-skinned beings called salamanders, which look similar to the common scaleless lizard-like amphibians that share their name. Elemental salamanders are sometimes visible as small balls of fire and have also been seen in the shape of tongues of flame that can run over fields and peer into dwellings. No fire is lit without their help. In fact, the salamander comes from the Greek word *salambe*, meaning 'fireplace'. These spirits control all manner of flame, lightning, explosions, volcanoes and combustion. Mostly they are active underground and internally within the body and mind. Salamanders evoke powerful emotional currents in humans, and stimulate fires of spiritual idealism and perception. Their energy is much like that of the Tarot Card, The Tower, assisting in the tearing down of the old and the building of the new - as fire can be both constructive and destructive in its creative expression.

The salamanders are the guardians of summer and Fire, and reside in the realm of passion, change, prophetic visions, personal power, inspiration and the inner child. They function in the physical body by aiding circulation and in maintaining proper body temperature, and working with the body's metabolism for greater health.

Fire elementals work with humans via heat, fire and flame. This includes everything from the flame of a candle to the ethereal flames and daily light of the Sun. They can be powerfully effective in healing work, but must be used carefully for such applications, as their energies are dynamic and difficult to control. They are almost always present when there is any healing going to occur. Fire provides us with warmth, fuel and heating, and voraciously destroys the old so new life can spring forth out of the ashes - it is the essence from which the legendary phoenix arises. Fire also represents the inner child, that place of innocence from which we all stem. As it gives rise to sexual fervour it is also the root of our creative spirits. The fire elementals can indeed awaken in us higher spiritual visions and aspirations. They strengthen and stimulate the entire auric field to enable easier attunement to and recognition of Divine forces within our lives.

The salamanders can be seen in the heart of fires, dancing like dragons in the flames, and this dragon symbology is used in many Eastern religions to pay homage to them. Salamanders love the Fire for it is nourished by it - yet it is so cold within itself that it cannot be harmed by the flames. They help blacksmiths in their task of forging mighty swords and armour, feeding strength into the flames to have it then yield into the blacksmith's purpose. And yet the salamander is a mighty and tenacious defender of Fire. Only the strongest powers can hold it at bay - it can then be a loyal ally and not an enemy to bar us on our quest. The King of Fire is Belenos or Djin, its archangel is Michael, its magickal tool is the wand (which calls down the spirits into form), and its sacred ceremonial stones are Yellow Topaz, Amber and Citrine.

INVOKING THE FIRE DEVAS

If you wish to increase your sexual prowess, inspiration or creativity, need some career or goal luck, are fearful of an imminent but necessary change or move, or you are in need of courage or energy to meet a challenge, ask the fire devas for their help.

You can encounter salamanders most easily in a bonfire or open hearth. Some see them as sparks or flashes of colour. Dragon-like beings that live within flames, you can see them coiling within the swirling and lapping heat of the flames, and watch others dance and crackle in the sparks. They also reside in every beam of sunlight and flow of electricity. If you do not have access to a proper fire, a candle can serve the same purpose: call upon their help by meditating upon a lit candle. Lighting several at once, particularly in the colours of red and orange, may heighten the power.

THE SOUTH DIRECTION'S CORRESPONDENCES

If you wish to work more with your particular element and direction, the following may help propel your wishes and magical journey:

Time of Day ★ Noon
Polarity ★ Male, negative
Exhortation ★ To dare
Musical Instruments ★ Brass instruments
Colours ★ Scarlet red
Season ★ Summer
Magical Instrument ★ Sword, dagger, athame
Altar Symbol ★ Lamp
Communion Symbol ★ Heat
Archangel ★ Michael
Human Sense ★ Sight

Art Forms ★ Dance, drama
Animals ★ Salamanders, lizards
Mythical Beast ★ Dragon
Magical Arts ★ Ritual
Guide Forms ★ Sun, protector god
Meditation ★ Bonfires
Images & Themes ★ Flames, volcanoes, midday Sun, walking through fire

HOW YOU CAN GET IN TOUCH WITH YOUR FIRE ENERGY

"To be alive is to be burning"

★ Use Fire energy when making wishes around the following: Banishing bad habits, enthusiasm, initiative, inspiration, playfulness, leadership, bringing out the inner child, courage, confidence, dynamic energy, psychic protection, passion and desire

★ In magical practices, Fire can be represented by a candle (red or yellow will strengthen its fiery association), a fireplace, smudge sticks, bonfires or, symbolically, a wand. The candle wax of a burning candle represents Fire's powers of change and transformation - melting as it burns, changing its shape and substance

★ The best days on which to employ Fire magic are Tuesday, ruled by the fiery Red Planet Mars, or a Sunday, ruled by the blazing Sun. If possible, choose midday when the Sun is at its zenith

★ Eat spicy, hot foods, such as chilli and cayenne, and use fiery spices and sauces

★ Burn a bridge, clean a slate

★ Write your wish/es down on a piece of red paper, then burn it to release the smoke along with its message into the Universe to be fulfilled

★ Spend time in the Sun every day if possible, and around fires of all kinds - stoves, candles, fireplaces, camp fires

★ Yellow and orange-coloured crystals will activate your connection with the element of Fire and enhance your creativity.

★ Practice candle magic

★ Drink green tea

★ Indulge in forms of caffeine such as coffee and chocolate, but do so moderately or you may become jittery, scattered and jumpy, and therefore render your inner Fire ineffective

★ Use supplements which are designed to support and believed to enhance your Fire energy, such as ginger, spirulina and ginseng. Some energy bars may also prove beneficial

★ Practice deep breathing and meditation exercises and disciplines, which help to increase and circulate energy and blood throughout your body

★ Meditate using the Fire mantra "Ram"

★ Indulge in sexual release regularly

★ Schedule and maintain an ongoing physical exercise routine

★ Learn and practice yoga

★ Create a 'fire ritual', during which you regularly 'burn' away something which needs releasing or banishing

★ Take an acting, drama or theatrics class - or better still, become an actor on camera or on stage!

★ Learn about Fire gods and goddesses, and how they can benefit you. The Hawaiian Fire goddess Pele, is a great place to start

★ Meditate on the Wands suit in the Tarot (the Wands suit represents the Fire element)

★ Express yourself regularly and freely, either through the expressive arts, social events, or even a journal

★ Be bold, brave and courageous, even when you are not feeling like it

★ Choose a challenge and rise to it

★ Build your confidence daily by listing three achievements or goals you have reached, no matter how seemingly small or large

★ Wear and surround yourself with the colours red and orange

★ Commit yourself to a bright future by creating a vision or dream, and maintain it by keeping track of your steps along the way

★ Think and act big. As Marianne Williamson said: "Our deepest fear is not that we are inadequate. Our deepest fear is that we are powerful beyond measure. It is our light, not our darkness, that most frightens us. Your playing small does not serve the world ... We are all meant to shine as children do ... And as we let our own lights shine, we unconsciously give other people permission to do the same." So be bold and shine!

★ When working with the Fire element in magical practice, stand at the South quarter of your magical space, as the South is its domain, and invite its living essence into your circle or space

★ Fire spirits are known by metaphysicians as salamanders, and they inspire passion, blessings, new life, creativity, and spiritual healing. With all this in mind, Fire signs would be wise to adopt one as their very own spirit guide!

YOUR MODE ★ CARDINAL

Each sign belongs to one of the three quadruplicities, Cardinal, Fixed and Mutable. If we closely examine the Earth's yearly cycle, we can form a very accurate picture of the nature of these quadruplicities, for they correspond directly with the manifestation of the seasons. Each season has three months: the first month brings the new phase of the cycle, the second month brings a concentration of the season's energy to its fullest expression, and the third month represents the transition from the current season to the next one. The astrological quadruplicities represent the three basic qualities in all life: creation (Cardinal), perseveration (Fixed) and destruction (Mutable). Every thing that is born, from a period of time to a human being, experiences a life and then dies. In this context, death can be taken to mean that the form of the energy changes; but the energy itself can never be annihilated, for form is mortal, whereas essence is immortal.

The Cardinal mode covers the signs Aries, Cancer, Libra and Capricorn, and is the most initiating and self-motivated group of the three modes, able to instigate and inspire beginnings; in other words, to "get the ball rolling." The Cardinal mode has an initiating action and quality, operating with ambition, enthusiasm, independence and enterprise. Forceful, opportunistic, and at times aggressive, you have the will to accomplish and creatively project yourself onto the world. You charge right in to get the job done - but you can fail just as spectacularly. Although you have a great start-up ability, tenacity and endurance are not your fortes, and you often don't follow things through to the end. If there is no crisis for you to tackle, you may even make one up just to create a challenge for yourself. You find it hard to be held under anyone's thumb and will always find a way to wriggle free to set off on your next quest. Your energies may be directed towards yourself, your home and family, or the wider world of career or society, but in any case it is difficult to divert your attention away from your chosen course. Cardinal signs have great drive, are self-motivated and would rather lead than follow. It is hard to influence you because you make your own firm decisions and believe that you know best. The Cardinal mode signifies beginnings, decision-making, boldness, courage, will, new starts, and initiations. You tend to be dynamic, authoritative, 'bossy', active, restless, involved, busy and energetic, and are determined initiators of goals and new purposes. The Sun's entry into the Cardinal signs indicates the beginning of seasons in the northern hemisphere: the start of Aries marks the Spring Equinox, the beginning of Libra the Autumn Equinox, the start of Cancer the Winter Solstice, and the beginning of Capricorn the Summer Solstice.

Aries is the most pioneering of the Cardinal quality; you are constantly trying to get in first and spark up new beginnings in whatever form they may take. Being a leader, and quite a forceful character, as well as being the only Fire Cardinal sign, gives you the edge and upper hand. Your self-confidence further assists your ascent up life's ladder.

YOUR RULING PLANET ★ MARS

The Great Warrior & Brave Crusader

Planetary Meditation
I am my Earth (my body),
and my Sky (my transcendence)
I am my Sun (my spirit),
and my Moon (my soul)
I am my Venus (my pleasure),
and my Jupiter (my faith)
I am my Mars (my courage),
and my Saturn (my lessons)
I am my Mercury (my thoughts),
and my Uranus (my truth)
I am my Neptune (my dreams),
and my Pluto (my transformation)

Each planet has its own distinctive and original meaning which, according to its position in the zodiac, combines with the qualities that are inherent in each of the twelve astrological signs. If a planet is your sign's ruler, however, it exerts a significant influence upon your life, regardless of its birth chart or zodiacal position.

Malefic ★ Associated with Drive, Passion, Aggression & Confidence ★ 687 Day Cycle

★ KEY WORDS ★
Action, Drive, Competition, Desire, Courage, Force, Vitality, Impulse, Bravery, Passion, Initiative, Sexuality, Anger, Power, Ego, Achievement, Ambition, Wilfulness, Vigour, Assertion, Confidence, Territoriality, Conquering

and Overcoming, Energy, Motivation, Aggression, Will, Masculinity, Confrontation, Battle, Enthusiasm, Virility, Heat, Dynamism

★ KEY CONCEPTS ★

★ The Inner Warrior ★
★ Ego in Action ★
★ Passion, Desire, Drive ★
★ Warfare, Weapons, Tools of Destruction ★
★ Fearlessness, Courage ★
★ Vitality, Vigour ★
★ Desire ★
★ The Fighting Spirit ★
★ The Slayer of Inner Demons ★
★ Animal & Survival Instincts ★

Day ★ Tuesday

Number ★ 9

Basic Energy & Magic ★ Action, Motivation

Colours ★ Strong Reds, Scarlet, Magenta, Autumnal Shades

Gods/Goddesses/Angel ★ Ares, Mars, Samael

Metals ★ Iron, Steel, Brass

Gems/Minerals ★ Ruby, Bloodstone, Malachite, Lodestone, Garnet, Flint, Carnelian, Hematite, Pyrite

Trees/Shrubs ★ Monkey-puzzle, Heather, Holly, Pine, Hawthorn

Flowers/Herbs ★ Nasturtium, Nettle, Allspice, Tobacco, Garlic

Wood ★ Mahogany
Fabric ★ Tweed

Animal ★ Tiger, Falcon, Wolf, Snake

Element ★ Fire

Zodiacal Signs ★ Aries, Scorpio

Zodiacal Influences ★ Rules Aries (Co-rules Scorpio); Exalted in Capricorn; Detriment Libra; Fall Cancer

Mars is nicknamed the Red Planet * due to its red-orange colour, and its brilliant appearance in the night sky. Forceful, fearless and daring, Mars governs the whole spectrum of traditionally 'masculine' concepts from sex to combat, strenuous activities, domination, leadership, and nerves-of-steel risk-taking. It is also known as the warrior planet, due to its ability to outlast and outdistance its adversaries. Bringing endurance, ambition, thrills and determination, when strongly placed in a natal chart it can add a touch of boldness and excitement to one's character. It brings movement, noise and plenty of activity to the area of life that its House placement in the horoscope indicates. Mars rules sharp instruments, fire and anything combustible, its sheer force can destroy matter, and hot-headed outbursts are likely when it is free to run rampant in one's life or psyche. Yet Mars can, conversely, bring zest, spirit, passion and energy to whatever it touches. Rather than limiting the interpretation of Mars to physical strength, the full meaning of the planet must be understood: it stands for the energetic power, the potential of action which is contained inside each of us, and the life forces which generate action, movement, behaviours, the assertion of our personality and the expression of our raw, spontaneous feelings.

It is easy to see why astrologers of medieval times observed the Red Planet with trepidation: it foretold war, plague and fever. Named after the Roman god of war and spring, Mars is the planet most concerned with the way we assert ourselves and what it is that drives us. He is always shown powerfully built and dressed for adventure and the battlefield.

Mars powers our activities and energies. Ariens (and to a large degree, Scorpios) get their energy and drive from the Red Planet. The mythical Mars was known for his courage and impetuosity on the battlefield and in the bedroom, and its natives also often leap impetuously into love and battle. Flying on the wings of passion, Martians can learn from disasters, and heed their planet's message: Act now; life is too short to waste time on regrets.

The glyph (or symbol) for Mars is pure masculinity, a circle with an arrow pointing upward, suggesting that Mars works on an entirely material plane. There are no crescent circles indicating spirit, as Mars deals with the here, now and immediate. The arrow is phallic, symbolising sexuality and direct action. It represents the masculine in biology and iron in physics. Mars also has an impressive history with all things warlike, which is reflected in its traditional glyph - a heavy metal helmet.

Mars is the secondary masculine principle in our natal chart, the 'male within'. It represents our directive energy the way we direct it and the targets we direct it towards, the urge for activity, masculinity, our survival impulse, the sexual instinct and drive, personal power, confidence, ego, achievement, progress, conquering fear and overcoming obstacles. The last of the personal planets, its position and condition shows how the principles of both action and desire are expressed, revealing the kinds of projects and battles we choose and how they are tackled. The adrenaline of the horoscope, Mars denotes the urge towards 'fight or flight' tendencies and indeed our mode of attack when threatened. Therefore, it is also connected with our basic energy, territoriality, personal power through wilful expression, self-mastery, vitality, drive, aspiration, assertiveness, activity, force, power, accomplishment, strength, ambition, competitiveness, conquest, passion, courage, unchecked emotion and anger. It indicates our impulse to act and to motivate.

The position of Mars in your birth chart determines how bold you are and reveals your competitive nature. It also indicates your energy levels, the way you use your energy, your levels of assertiveness, the type of bravery you possess, how you use your courage and initiative, and reflects your passion and desires. Mars shows the nature of the challenges you are likely you face and your ability to confront them. Your sexual desires also come under the rule of Mars and in a female's birth chart it often shows the kind of men she is attracted to, and in a male's birth chart it shows his attitude towards other men and his masculinity. It is also associated with fighting, conflicts, arguments and hostility, and how you conduct yourself when faced with these. Its position also shows your basic sexual nature, styles and tastes, how you express your anger, what makes you angry and how you instinctively react.

Mars's element tells us how we replenish our stores of energy; its sign tells us what turns us on in laughter, play and sex. People with a strong Mars in their chart are go-getters, assertive, courageous, need to win, need to come first, love a challenge and are unafraid of confrontation. Too much Mars influence can make one contentious, quarrelsome, overly competitive, prone to accidents, aggressive and even violent. Concerned with raw sexuality, heated feelings and to some extent, our instinctive actions, at his best he can employ a well-trained inner 'army' that directs its energies towards efficiency, well-used power and discipline; however, at his worst he can run wild and rampant on an undisciplined, impulsive foray of pillage, violence and cruelty. The former, channelled energy brings out the courageous and assertive aspect of the masculine principle - confrontation is direct and confident, action is strong and effective. Mars commands respect when used harmoniously, but he only needs a slight loss of power or control for his energy to erupt into disorder, aggression and acute rage. But although Mars has assumed many roles over the ages and is best known as a warrior and protector, he also has a bellicose nature which reveals a gentler side, in which he also plays the lover and provider **. He is a strong leader in times of crisis, and is a defender of the weak.

Named after the god of war, Mars is the planet most concerned with the way we assert ourselves and what it is that drives us. As the archetype of the warrior, it powers our activities and energies. It sees things in black and white, chooses a goal and decides upon the most direct path to it. All that matters to Mars is the objective, and, lacking perspective and patience, he will surmount and crash through any obstacles in his way to get to it. Considering Mars is the motivating force through which we are impelled to act, he operates accordingly - quickly and without forethought - when the urge strikes, and nothing will stop him. Therein contains the reason Mars is so dangerous when uncontrolled in one's horoscope. However, giving us strength of will and direction, he can also be used constructively, even when seemingly uncontrolled, as he signifies the ultimate power and purpose we need to slay our inner demons. But because Mars excels at achieving immediate aims he is not capable of long-term or strategic planning and generally relies on force and aggression rather than negotiation, finesse or diplomacy. So whether we are working on ourselves, or battling with others, the fight will be won quickly or not at all, as Mars's confrontations simply burn out over long periods of time, and manifest in other undesirable conditions such as exhaustion or depression. If used for good, Mars can enable us to 'go to war on ourselves' and emerge triumphant.

Mars is a planet which operates strongly when we are young, as it is a basic energy used in the search for our identity. While its aggression and feeling comes from a primitive part of ourselves, in maturity it is more likely to be either controlled or sublimated so the function of Mars is bound to change during our lifetimes. The sign in which Mars is found in birth is particularly important, since it helps to indicate one's basic drive and force, and how this energy will be used. Its relationship to the Sun is also of vital importance. In astrological terminology, it could be said that Mars should take its direction from the Sun, and fight for the cause of personal consciousness. Since the Sun is regarded as the vital power underlying the self, the multi-dimensional, centred individuality which is the goal of all spiritual work, when the Self (the Sun) directs the warrior (Mars), magnificent things are possible.

Ariens who are under this powerful planet's rulership, are energetic, fearless, good fighters, quick-tempered, impulsive and independent. It also lends you plenty of ardour and impulse but you may lack self-discipline, patience, restraint, grace and tact. It also gives you a distaste for regimentation and slow-moving or drawn out situations.

The Gauquelins, who undertook the most highly acclaimed and recognised statistical research in the field of astrology, found that a prominent Mars in the horoscope, produced individuals who excelled in the fields of military, medicine, business and science; conversely, Mars was *least* prominent for musicians, artists and writers. Further studies concluded that Mars is marked in the birth charts of 'iron-willed' sports stars, and there had to be more to this correlation than mere coincidence. What was perhaps even more notable was where Mars was placed in the charts of champions and crusaders of their fields: the areas where Mars had just risen (Twelfth House) or culminated (Ninth House). Therefore, it could be said that the strength of this planet depends not upon the *sign* in which it is placed at birth, nor the planetary aspects involved, but the sector of the chart in which it appears. People with such prominent Martian influence in their charts, are encouraged to undertake sports and regular physical activities, in order to blow off the enormous amount of steam that can build up within them, for failing to do this may allow dis-eases of inflammation or fever to manifest and cause havoc if their characteristic pent-up energy is held in for too long.

Mars is the polar opposite and husband of Venus. Just as Venus, daughter of the Moon, represents the feminine archetype, Mars, son of the Sun, is the active male archetype. Taurus and Libra, the signs ruled by Venus, are directly opposite Scorpio and Aries, the domains of Mars. And when these forces unite, the result can be likened to *love in action*.

Mars is the planet that governs our active self. It influences our physical energy levels and the vitality behind our actions. To express our personality, we need to be assertive and impose our choices and initiatives. This ability to act is the way we demonstrate our enthusiastic zest for life, make our wishes come true and satisfy our desires.

However, because Mars is an indiscriminate fighter and battles for its own sake, fighting on either side with equal zest, sometimes you need your discerning Mercury to show him the road you want him to take. Mars is the great achiever. He can and will perform any task you set for him. In order to attain your goals, you must let him know exactly what you desire - the more details you give him, the less he will be led astray. His force will forge ahead to bring your wishes to manifestation for as long as you hold the image firmly in mind, maintain your focus, and continue to work at it. And *work* is the operative word here, as Mars is no dreamer.

Mars is associated with red, abrasive, fevers, soldiers, guns, Tuesday, vanguards, weaponry, brutal, bullets, assault, mutilation, impulsive, threats, stoves, blisters, attack, savagery, conquests, smelting, spears, axes, incision, surgeons, feuds, rebellion, brave, stings, gymnastics, breakages, bullfights, accidents, sandpaper, butchers, swords, temper, military, construction, explosives, steel, discord, hot instruments, quarrels, blazing, murder, sabres, boilermakers, daring, acrobatics, stamina, vigour, boxing, haste, destruction, whips, action, rasps, surgery, headaches, pins, slaughter, hoodlums, adventure, incinerators, forks, physical exercise, punctures, boldness, dentists, missiles, inflammation, rash, challenges, urgent, stakes, artillery, furnaces, strength, aggression, dagger, agitators, firebugs, pioneers, violence, singeing, welding, ammunition, rugged, brawls, hardware, strife, carpenters, carving, assassins, excitement, amputation, spikes, competitive sports, danger, mechanics, imprudence, emergencies, injury, turbulent, helmets, anger, antagonism, bullies, shooting, fighting, cannons, thugs, pistols, rifles, scalpels, heat, armaments, cuts, foundries, rape, friction, muscles, armed forces, enmity, arsenal, firearms, scalds, contests, initiative, peril, burns, arrows, barbers, sharp, effort, police, prowess, battles, engraving, tournaments, regiments, rage, bayonets, belligerence, hostility, scorching, conflict, impatience, toasted, bites, chisels, energy, defiance, saws, blacksmiths, ovens, fire-fighters, scratches, implements, sharp tools, torpedoes, instruments, combustion, invaders, iron, defence, irritation, machinery, masculine, scissors, opponents, pain, radiators, rams, combat, courage, crimes of violence, darts, engineers, Fire, scars, virility and of course, war. I'm sure you get the idea!

This Martian energy and influence, throughout your whole life, gives Ariens the gifts of independence, assertiveness, self-confidence, boldness, heroism, passion, directness, courage, initiative, willpower, determination, ambition, enterprise and strength. Too much of this Martian energy can make one confrontational, brutal, domineering, aggressive, blatant, hot-headed, rash, contentious, argumentative, quick-tempered, foolhardy, quarrelsome, competitive, insensitive, domineering, ruthless, accident-prone, bossy, careless and demanding. But the Mars-inspired Arien spirit will always triumph over any odds; after all, your motto is "I Am," because quite simply, you just *are*. Mars is an energy which, in its primal state, is without a sense of direction, but when connected with a purpose, it can accomplish victorious feats. How will *you* use your phenomenally powerful Martian influence?

* Red, as well as being the colour of lust and passion, has strong links with Mars by virtue of red being the colour that appears when tempers rise to the boiling point, as well as being the colour of blood (spilt by battle)

** Mars has earned a bad reputation for being an 'aggressor', but the Romans highly esteemed Mars and attributed many positive qualities to him. He was a giver of fertility, a god of nature, a protector of herds and fields, and a great inspiration to all new ideas and projects. They even dedicated the first month, the period of the vernal equinox signifying the coming of spring, and named it in his honour - hence the word, 'March'.

YOUR HOUSE IN THE HOROSCOPE ★ THE FIRST HOUSE

ASCENDANT - ASC - Cusp of the First House.
The Ascendant is the degree of the zodiac rising on the eastern horizon at the moment of birth. It signifies the point of self-awareness: "I am."

The First House is the first thing others notice about you. In a literal house, it would be the front door. It shows your outer personality and the impression you give on first meeting others.

A house is one of the twelve sections dividing the terrestrial globe, viewed from a precise time and geographical place, into sectors from the poles to the horizon. The horoscope, or birth chart, is divided into these twelve sections called houses. Each house governs a different area or 'department' of life, such as relationships, career, leisure and even karma. The reason for this division of the Earth into houses can be understood when we consider that the Sun's rays affect us differently in the morning, at noon and at night, and also in summer and winter, and if we study the cause, we will readily observe that it is the angle at which the ray strikes us or the Earth which produces that difference in effect.

Similarly, with the stellar rays, astrologers have observed that a child born at or near midday, when the Sun's rays strike the birthplace from the Tenth House, has an improved chance of public or career advancement in life than one born after sunset. By similar observations and tabulations, it has been found that the other planetary rays affect the various departments of life when their ray is projected through the other houses, and therefore each house is said to 'rule' or govern certain departments of the human life experience

The First House, ruled by Aries, is the house of individuality, the projected self, incarnation, self-image, basic approach to life, physical characteristics and personal appearance, one's reaction to the immediate environment, outer mannerisms, identity and persona. This house, also known as the Ascendant, is commonly known as our 'social mask', and is often the first impression others have of us. It represents how directly we express our individuality, our outer behaviour, how we come across before others truly know our inner drives and selves.

As a Fire sign, this is one of the three Houses of Life, and is an all-important 'angular' House, being the Ascendant, meaning that it forms one of the four significant angles of the birth chart (the other three being the Fourth House or Imum Coeli, the Seventh House or Descendent, and the Tenth House or Midheaven). But where Leo is concerned with life on an interpersonal level and Sagittarius with life on a transpersonal, or wider-reaching level, Aries and the First House are concerned with life on a personal level.

It has been said that if your Sun sign is the message that you have to give to the world, then your Ascendant or First House is the *style* in which you deliver that message. The First House is that set of characteristics that you present to the outside world, and to which other people perceive initially, before they get to know the 'authentic' core you, your Sun sign. As such, it is an 'astrological overcoat', your outer manner, and what others see first - that all-important first impression you make on other people.

The First House covers our levels of self-awareness, self-absorption and self-protection, our social mannerisms, self-expression, the image we present to others and the world, our basic personality and temperament, beginnings, self-discovery, how others see us (first impressions), and what we may hide behind. Other exoteric and esoteric keywords include: the self, ego, anima, projected image, expression of inner motivations, soul purpose, initial approach to life, and the aura. It is connected with your overall temperament, vitality, mannerisms, and the general course of your life. Planets and signs in this house pervade the whole of life, describing particular expectations and the way in which interaction with the outside world takes place.

On a physical level, it shows our constitution, physical appearance and build, health, disposition, wellbeing, and the level of physical vitality or energy available to us. The First House indicates the part/s of the body which are chiefly vulnerable to illness, weakness or injury, as well as correlating to the spark of life and the resultant energy that's released into the world. It describes our physical birth and physical body, the circumstances surrounding our birth and the reception our arrival engendered, and thereafter our mode of encountering the world. The Ascendant marks the moment when you joined the world, and the nature of any planet within the first house, or within 8 degrees either side of it, describes the impact you made. As well, it describes the projection of the Self into the immediate environment. As a sensitive chart angle point, this is arguably one of the most important of the houses, as it is a vital link in life, showing how vital we are.

The importance of the Ascendant/First House cannot be over-emphasised, for it is the most sensitive part of the horoscope, colouring your whole personality. It reveals the way in which you relate to those around you, and shows who you are and how you approach life. The signs and planets that fall into this house show the aspects that are most valuable in realising your unique identity. It provides insights into the conditions of your early environment that shaped you into the person you are today and may become in the future.

The First House describes our characteristic quirks, how we come across on a superficial level, how we *wish* to appear, self-image, public persona, instinctive initial outer behaviours, and habits. In fact, the Ascendant is almost, if not equally, as important as your Sun sign, and offers further insights into the rich tapestry of your individuality. Any planet which is found on or near (within 8 degrees either side of) the Ascendant, will play a strongly significant role in defining your character.

The First House describes character, personal inclinations, passions, as well as the fundamentals of fortune. If this house contains a number of planets or chart points, it may be suggested there is an abundance of talents and versatility.

Overall, as a house of beginnings, this house is considered our birthing point, how we 'emerge' into the world (both literally and metaphorically), our social mask, outlook, idiosyncrasies, persona, our image, our defences, and our birth story. Most importantly, it is what we appear to be but not who we actually are, concerning what is visible. It is a dual lens, through which others see you, and also through which you focus your true character to the outside world. It can also act as a 'filter', through which you assimilate your experience of life. Through the sign on its cusp, it describes your basic nature and the manner in which you approach your goals in life, the type of path you'll take towards your ultimate destiny.

YOUR OPPOSITE SIGN ★ LIBRA
WHAT YOU CAN LEARN FROM THE SCALES

If we look at the zodiac, we can see that it can be broadly divided into two hemispheres, this division being based on the natural division of the year by the two equinoxes. Astrologers often refer to the first six signs, the hemisphere in which the day predominates (the days being longer in the spring and summer months), as the Personal Sphere of Experience, and the second six signs, the hemisphere in which nights are longer, as the Social Sphere of Experience. These two halves of the zodiac perfectly balance and complement each other, and each individual 'personal' zodiac sign has something to teach its directly opposite 'social' zodiac sign. To generalise, the signs of the personal sphere tend to experience life through a type of self-projection and self-interest which is often socially uncomplicated, unsophisticated or naïve. Their objective is to learn greater social awareness and thereby integrate themselves with the larger, more universal human collective.

On the other hand, the signs of the social sphere are prone to experience life through the use of their more developed social consciousness. In essence, the personal signs (Aries, Taurus, Gemini, Cancer, Leo, Virgo) usually provide stimulation and new energy to their environment, while the social, more universal signs (Libra, Scorpio, Sagittarius, Capricorn, Aquarius, Pisces) provide experience, opportunities for wider expression, and give a more broad-minded approach and perspective to their surroundings.

Each sign in a pair seeks and is attracted to the qualities of its complementary opposing sign. Aries desires to obtain the balanced judgement of Libra, and Libra wishes to have more of the self-direction and independence of Aries. Aries is concerned with awareness of the self, and Libra primarily concerns itself with awareness of others. In essence, Aries dwells within the realm of self-projection through *individual* impulse, and Libra within the realm of self-projection through *social* impulse.

Although the word 'opposite' conjures up feelings of separateness and differences, the astrological polarities should not be seen as two signs in conflict with each other - their positive expression is to create a natural balance and equilibrium. Each sign has something to learn from its opposite, but also has a contribution to make towards the other sign's more evolved expression. The First (Aries) and the Seventh (Libra) House polarity is concerned with awareness of self, versus awareness of others.

Positive and Cardinal, this polarity in some ways epitomises the battle of the sexes. Venus seeks union, Mars acts independently, but as with relationships between male and female, each needs the other. The strong individuality of Aries needs to learn the balance and cooperation offered by Libra. Self-orientation and the desire for freedom can mellow through the experience of compromise in a relationship with another person. But Libra's social involvement and its feeling of loss that exists without the 'other half' of the partnership, may lead to uncertainty and dependence. Libra is gently strengthened if it can develop the qualities of initiative, greater independence, and single-mindedness characterised by the self-interested and ego-driven Aries.

The two houses ruled by Aries and Libra are the First and Seventh houses. These show your individual self-image and how you relate in close contact with other people. The First House is concerned with awareness of self, while the Seventh House is concerned with awareness of others.

In any personal relationship (Seventh House), you will be seeking qualities (consciously or unconsciously) which will complement your own personality (First House) or which are needed to fill some psychological gap in your character. The signs and planets connected with these houses will show what these are.

The bold, self-assertive, self-centred individual (Aries) needs to become more aware of others, and to develop a capacity for objective cooperation with them in relationships (Libra).

To evolve to your fullest potential, Aries needs to learn how to be spontaneous without ignoring the needs of others; to be a role model of self-confidence; to lead without being bossy or overpowering; to put yourself first only when it is leading others along their own ultimate paths by your shining example. These are all virtues you can learn from the gentler, subtler and more balanced Libra.

Your karmic goal is to develop the Self unselfishly and to serve others with less hesitation, a hesitation which has stemmed from your fear of being tied down or committed to a person or a cause, and also your incessant need to always be on the move and seeking new, stimulating, novel activities. In essence, you need to selflessly share your talents and abilities with others.

Aries relates to confidence, independence, and a desire to follow one's path. It also relates to the over-development of over-competitiveness and a desire to win. The lesson comes through learning that true success comes through abandoning the ego and cooperating with others. Listening to others is something else you may not be used to doing, and you even find it irritating when you feel it hinders your progress or stifles your ego. However, empty loneliness will result if you refuse to heed this lesson. It is important to remember that the ego must only ever be your servant, not your master.

The Aries spirit has the great ability to empower others: if, and only *if*, you can abandon your self-serving ways in true Libran spirit, and energise the wishes of other people by listening to what they want rather than thinking you know what is best for them. Working purely from unenlightened self-serving motives will only doom your efforts. Therefore, Libra can teach you that intrinsically linked to the unfoldment and fulfilment of your destined potential is the need to learn how to relate lovingly to others, particularly in partnerships. You must move yourself into an attitude that embraces others, takes their interests into account, and recognises that there are consequences in actions. The power of love and relating is what you are destined to learn from your cosmic partner Libra, and set about understanding and implementing it into your experiences. Joy will result from selfless giving, as Libra will strongly attest: after all, it is his greatest attribute. Your life will be further enriched by learning another lesson from your opposite: the bringing of art, beauty, music or the simple nobility of being, into other people's lives. In essence, you are the leader/warrior who has all the potential to uplift others, and become a true 'way-shower'. Developing diplomacy and courtesy, along with the arts of sharing and cooperating, not only lights the way, but adds to your considerable charm. You can also learn modesty and humility from the Scales.

You are largely characterised by your impatience and your constant need to be doing something. Most of this activity is based around self-serving interests and issues of control. You are convinced that you alone are able to take quick action, know what needs to be done and how it should be done. While true that you are endowed with sound energetic resources, a fierce, headstrong nature which cuts straight to the point, courage and an enviable ability to act, you can often take this too far and become domineering. Libra's naturally calm demeanour, cooperative skills and diplomacy help to temper these traits. Libra will show you a gentler path to follow: that of sharing, delegating and patience.

Part of your incessant need to lead and charge straight in, stems from trust - or the lack of it. You don't naturally trust that anyone can get the job done better than you can, which makes you anxious, frustrated and unbalanced. Libra can teach you to learn to trust others, acquire inner balance, and most importantly of all, to reflect before making a decision or rushing in. This will make you more selective, more efficient, less intimidating, and give you more steady footing.

Aries can be quite childish and egocentric. Libra has overcome all karmic lessons associated with these traits, and is now in a place of more mature standing when it comes to relationships. Your opposite Libra has much to teach you when it comes to relating to other people, and can help you to adapt better to others. So strap in, get comfortable, and enjoy the ride through the foreign world of give-and-take relationships. You will learn a lot from your opposite sign, and ideally, will start applying that Libran wisdom sooner than later.

Overall, the Arien experience is one of well-developed, even epic independence and a strong sense of the individual self. Although you have an indestructible demeanour, and have achieved this through arduous effort, an iron will and a fierce determination, these strong feelings of self-reliance have led you to believe that you don't really need anyone or anything; that is, until a crisis or series of challenges in your life forces you to see how crucial other people and relationships actually are. These are times when you must learn, through the opposing but highly complementary influence of the Libran, how to use your immense personal strength in subtler ways. Although your selfishness is largely unconscious, you have trouble letting go of the need to command and control, which have manifested in your close-mindedness and opinionated attitudes. Release your impatient restlessness and start taking the balanced middle way; your destiny awaits once you overcome the weaknesses highlighted in you by your easy going opposite, the perfectly balanced and moderate Scales.

Ultimately, you need to come out of your self-serving behaviour and shine a light upon the way ahead for others to find their way also; you need to start with relationships, and begin pouring as much attention into their maintenance as you do to yourself, in true Libra style! And you can be guaranteed that as you come out from behind the mask of your ego, your relationships and the people within them will thank you - and perhaps even shower you with the praise, recognition and attention you so seek.

WHAT THE SCALES CAN ULTIMATELY TEACH THE RAM

Release ★ The 'me first' mentality, aggression, battle, impatience, desire to intervene, hot-headedness, bossiness, impetuosity, childish behaviour, impulsivity

Embrace ★ The peaceful warrior, the power of partnership, graceful socialising, patience, inner balance, relational harmony, impartiality, sense of justice, better judgement, reflection, agreement, union, choosing your battles

Libra is relationship-oriented, dependent upon others, strives for equality, justice and fairness, is cooperative, accommodating, develops committed and mutually satisfying relationships, is law-abiding, appeasing, attempts to be liked, is tactful, flattering, poised, flattering, placid, cultivates loving relationships, weighs up alternatives, evaluates, delays action, is considerate, objective, aware of all points of view, strives for balance, peace and harmony, avoids conflict, and is harmonising and mediating.

Libra can therefore teach you how to consider the 'other' in relationships with more heart and soul, how to be less 'me'-oriented and become more 'others'-oriented, to integrate your true Self in relationships rather than remaining separate, to be less independent and more inter-dependent, to learn the art of cooperation, to serve others and be more aware and interested in other people, to become more graceful, and to more fully appreciate and incorporate peace, harmony and balance through being still and reflective.

MAGIC, DRAWING, ATTRACTION, SPELLS, RITUALS, WISHING & POWER

A Note on the Universe

Within each of us resides the merging of the Sun and the Moon, the dance of the constellations, the vibrations of the planets, and the vast microcosm and macrocosm of the entire *Universe*. Uni means 'one' and Verse means 'song'; therefore, the word Universe literally means 'One Song'. If you learn to tune yourself in, you can even hear it!

What is Magic?

Magic is a kind of special energy that is beyond description, and like most kinds of energy it has its own rules and ways of being manipulated. It remains an elusive term, and no definition has ever really found universal acceptance. Attempts to separate it from superstition, religion and other-worldly phenomena on the one hand, and 'science' on the other, are ridden with difficulties. However slippery the term 'magic' might be, there is a general agreement that most of us wish for more of its presence in our lives and often fall short of achieving this wish.

Those performing spells, 'asking the Universe', wishing, praying, or undertaking rituals, are using this very special energy to draw things to them. Learning to manipulate energy in these ways is never hard (and shouldn't be), but it can be complex and does require knowledge, practice, creativity, patience and above all, imagination. Most of us use simple magic every day, whether by saying little prayers, making wishes, visualising, and exchanging - sending out and receiving - good, positive or hopeful vibes. When you understand that all the forces and magic you need are *within* you, and you learn to *believe* in that power, you are then able to make all manner of changes to your life and, most importantly, yourself.

Magic is an invisible force which connects and permeates everything. Every thought you have and every action you take, will affect the strength of this force, and can be influenced and directed towards a specific purpose by using certain means. The most important of these are your intentions, facing in the direction of your desired outcome, your will and your *belief* that it works. The more you want something to happen, and the clearer you can visualise the desired outcome, the stronger your will and feelings towards it will be, ensuring an avalanche of amazing people, events and circumstances will flow into your experiences, gathering speed, momentum and power as it nears your goal or dream.

The Universe (or whichever higher power you believe in) works for us and through us. Ideas are given to us but they must be carried out *through* us, in the form of asking or acting or performing a ritual or casting a specific spell. The Universe's abundance is your abundance, and it flows through your mind into manifestation. The Universe or Divine Being in which you believe, gives you the necessary ideas and clothes them with all that is needed to bring them into form when we ask *believing*.

Based on ancient human beliefs, systems and superstitions, declaring what you want and acting out your deepest desires can actually help to make things happen. Magical ideas include the notion that thought affects matter and that the trained imagination can alter the physical world, that all aspects of the Universe are interdependent and that we can discover connections and correspondences between everyday occurrences and cosmic, or Divine, energies. A miracle or a wish coming true can suggest something is going on that extends beyond the laws of nature, that something unseen has occurred; but just because we cannot see it or touch it, it doesn't mean it's not there. Magic exists, especially if you truly believe it does, but science is so far incapable of capturing its essence or the rationale behind it. Personally, I prefer to leave that task to the higher powers of the Universe.

To help your dreams come true and to use your inborn power to its full effect, you can employ boosters based on the special energies and qualities of your Sun sign. These 'boosters' are chosen to be in alignment with the purpose of a particular goal, and contain energies of their own which will enhance the strength of your spell, prayer, ritual or 'asking'. Specific magical energies can be invoked by carrying out a spell or ceremony using specific herbs or colours, or on a particular day of the week, according to either your Sun sign (to heighten the power of the asking), and/or that is in sympathy with that for which you are asking (I have included days of the week for other Sun signs and spell types).

Some materials and boosters you can use to increase the power, magic or energy in any area of your life include: candles, wish lists (written on an appropriate piece of paper written with a specially-chosen writing tool), symbols, affirmations, chants, incense, herbs and flowers, locations, colours, days of the week, elements, crystals and gemstones, animal symbols, charms, talismans, amulets, gods and goddesses, essential oils, planetary hours and your Solar totem animals. All are covered, some more briefly than others, for your very special Sun sign to radiate the energy to powerfully draw your wildest dreams towards you!

Overall, it pays to remember that the Universe (or whatever higher power/s or force/s you happen to believe in) creates *through* you that to which you give your attention. What you contemplate becomes the law of your being, and through your pure unwavering belief, is eventually brought through to manifestation on the material plane. What you think about is entirely up to you. But just be mindful that whatever you think about the most becomes your dominant thought, then your main point of attraction, and is ultimately magnified until it becomes your reality or your experience. So choose your thoughts with care. And to quote Ralph Waldo Emerson, "Be careful what you set your heart upon, for it will surely be yours." I carry a copy of this beautiful prophecy in my purse as its words resonate so strongly with me. In other words, be mindful about what you're wishing for, for you will most probably get it, whether it's good or bad - magic, after all, doesn't discriminate. Just make your dominant thoughts good ones, and you will attract everything you set your heart and intentions upon. Good luck!

ASTROLOGY & MAGIC

"Everyone practices magic, whether they realise it or not, for magic is the art of attracting particular influences, events and situations within human life. Magic is a natural phenomenon because the Universe is reflexive, responding to human thoughts, aspirations and desires …"
David Fideler, *Jesus Christ, Sun of God*

Astrology is the most sublime of the occult * sciences, while at the same time it is one of the most practical for everyday application, for it divines the human soul itself. The cosmos, particularly the patterns that formed across it at the exact moment we were born, indicates the road along which our mental and spiritual endowments are likely to impel us, therefore enabling us to prepare in advance for life's battles, pitfalls, milestones, celebrations and of course to make the utmost of opportunities. Such is the magic of the human mind, that it can 'see' into the future and relive the past without having to be physically present in either, and when combined with astrological *knowing*, particularly the knowing that springs from understanding some of the dynamics of our natal chart, however basic, our inner - and outer - magic can be lifted to phenomenal heights.

In ancient times, not only was astrology the ardent study of the most learned and powerful minds, but among the masses of ordinary people its authority and guidance was accepted and followed without question. How this powerful knowledge was used was - and still is - up to the individual, but all who used it applied it to their perceived advantage.

As primitive humans observed the skies, no doubt they gradually realised that certain stars upon which their fate depended accompanied the seasons, or certain times of the year. They may also have reasoned that if governed their fate, they also governed their bodies, and it is therefore conceivable that the skies were associated with Divine influence. Certain celestial influences were believed to emanate from the thirty-six decans of the signs, and the mysterious but apparent effect that they exercised upon humans were thought to be due to a subtle ether shed by the heavenly stars and spheres on the Earth, that affected not only people, but also other animals, plants and minerals. For the ancient mind, linking magic with astrology may have also provided a much needed sense of predictability and patterns.

Early astrologers named and made associations with the imaginary divisions of the twelve signs and the twelve houses, and people born under a certain sign were said to inherit to an extent, its properties and nature. They also believed that the influence of the planets and stars corresponded with the medicinal properties of certain plants and minerals. They therefore asserted that the influence of a star or planetary position would affect the type of medicine or healing they would offer a subject to attain the most beneficial outcome. Throughout the writings of early philosophers and theorists, there is constant reference to this unmistakable mystic connection between the seven known planets and Earthly affairs and ailments. The seven metals were connected with the seven planets, to which the seven colours and the seven transformations were added. So the alchemist came to share the astrological doctrine that each planet ruled some mineral: The Sun ruled gold, the Moon silver, Mars iron, Venus copper, Saturn lead, Jupiter tin, and Mercury quicksilver. Consequently, in alchemical symbolism the same sign came to represent the metal and its corresponding planet.

In subsequent years, astrology became closely related to alchemical knowledge and development, and the alchemist came to be regarded as an authority not only on the transmutation of metals, but also on astrology and magic. This goes some of the way to explaining how magic and divination, which had always been inseparably bound up with astrology, came to be associated with alchemy. In all the occult sciences, the supreme power was believed to be in the stars above, and from their mysterious emanations all the metals, crystals, minerals, plants and herbs derived their special properties over time. Further, as alchemy became ever more spiritual and concerned with more abstract and philosophical concepts, eventually it was considered that the transmutation of lead into gold was simply a metaphor for the transformation of base matter, in this case the human soul, into a much purer and higher state of wisdom and being.

The Sun and Moon were believed to have greater influence over the human body than all the other heavenly bodies, and to exert their influence in various ways whenever they entered a certain sign of the zodiac. And although the Moon was traditionally regarded as the most important factor of a horoscope, the Sun has come into its own in later centuries, with the result that almost everyone knows their Sun sign but only those who have delved deeper are aware of the sign their natal Moon falls in. For this reason, I have chosen to focus this book series on the twelve Sun signs, as this is what the majority of people are most familiar with.

The following pages contain methods, energies, materials and objects which may be used to increase the magic and power of your Sun sign's influence upon you. Precious stones, flowers, colours and so on, are regarded as having a potent effect upon good fortune by attuning your mind to receive harmonious vibrations from the astral forces that surround you.

Finally, a basic working knowledge of basic astronomy and astrology is an asset when working with luck, abundance, wealth and personal power. You can attract more of these things when you align yourself with the workings of the wider Universe, the movement of the Sun, stars, Moon and planets and become aware of the correlations between the outer cycles of the skies and the inner cycles within yourself. Also, for those who are knowledgeable about Moon phases, equinoxes and solstices, a world of lucky possibilities can also magically open up to you. You don't need to know about astrology's deepest complexities to understand how everything interrelates; just learning the basics will give you an edge - and hopefully the following lucky tips will provide you with at least a small glimpse into the insights gleaned from your Sun sign, which I am certain will endow upon you the potential for amazing results to manifest in your life - and maybe even a step up one further rung towards the heavens!

* The word 'occult' comes from the Latin *occultus*, which literally means 'knowledge of the hidden'.

USING COLOURS, CRYSTALS, DEITIES, PLANTS, FOODS & MATERIAL SUBSTANCES FOR INCREASING POWER & MAGNETISING MAGIC

Alchemist, reformer and mystic Henry Cornelius Agrippa, born in 1486, in his principal work, *On Occult Philosophy*, expressed his belief in the doctrines of astrology and in the theory that the spirit of the world exists in the body of the world, just as the human spirit exists in the body of man. He contended that this spirit also abounds in the celestial bodies and descends in the rays of stars, so that the things influenced by their rays become conformable to them. By this spirit every occult property is conveyed into metals, stones, herbs and animals, through the Sun, Moon and planets, and even through the stars beyond and higher than the planets. A firm believer in the efficacy of charms, he stated that they may "be worn on the body bound to any part of it or hung around the neck, changing sickness into health or health into sickness." I believe the same effect could be applied to wishing and the thinking of positive thoughts, to mean, "Changing thoughts and dreams into manifest reality." He also recommended that these charms be worn in the form of finger rings (that have been created using the materials in agreement and harmony with your Sun Sign's magical energy).

Material substances are connected with abstract purposes by a complex but highly usable and accessible system of correspondences. Use these time-honoured connections in your own spells and wishes to magnetise your desires to you. The following pages will give you some materials, energies, forces and ideas you can summon the power of in order to enhance your magic and luck.

PLANETS

The Planetary influence of the day is important when 'asking' for something. If you are wishing for luck, for example, try working with your Sun sign's inherent energies combined with the perfect day of the week for it. So an Arien might try using his natural enthusiasm and eagerness, to ask for greater luck on a Thursday, which is Jupiter's Day and Jupiter is renowned for being a lucky planet, or better still, ask for luck on a Tuesday, which is Mars's day, planetary ruler of Aries, at the time of day when Jupiter's influence is at its most powerful (information about planetary hours for each day of the week can be found on the Internet or in books on the subject, and can be complex and detailed. It is an art to memorise the correct times, days and energies for the correct spells. If you are determined enough to achieve your dream or goal however, you will be determined enough to put in the research to do it properly!) On the next page you will find a very simplified list of the days of the week and their meanings.

DAYS OF THE WEEK & THEIR POWERS

MONDAY ★ Moon
Cancer

The Divine feminine, changes, intuition, emotions, secrets, dealing with women, purity, goodness, perfection, unity, psychic ability, magic, spirituality, invoking a goddess's or angel's guidance, anything that fluctuates, contracts, increases or decreases.

TUESDAY ★ Mars
Aries & Scorpio

Enthusiasm, competition, passion, energy, courage, protection, victory, anything requiring assertiveness, standing up for yourself, or a 'fighting spirit', determination, vitality, sexuality, self-confidence, men's power, men's mysteries, drive, ambition, achievement, triumph, masculinity.

WEDNESDAY ★ Mercury
Gemini & Virgo

Education, travel, exams, study, communication, making connections, thinking, dealing with siblings, writing and speaking, knowledge, learning, adaptability, charm, youth, absorbing information.

THURSDAY ★ Jupiter
Sagittarius & Pisces

Increase and expansion of anything (remember to be careful what you wish for), luck, growth, influence, worldly power, accomplishment, fulfilment, gambling, philosophy, higher education, abundance, optimism.

FRIDAY ★ Venus
Taurus & Libra

Love, luxury, the arts, indulgence, beauty, marriage, money, prosperity, fertility, women's power, women's mysteries, grace, charm, appeal, hope, pleasure, decorating, self-worth, self-esteem, personal values, business partnerships, romance, creativity, sharing, bonding.

SATURDAY ★ Saturn
Capricorn & Aquarius

Long-term goals, career, institutions, establishments, security, investments, karma, reversal, structure, protection, solitude, privacy, determination, ending, blocking, renewing, transforming, anything to do with the public.

SUNDAY ★ Sun
Leo

All-purpose, success, wishes, generosity, happiness, optimism, spirit/essence, recognition, health, vitality, material wealth, invoking a god's aid or guidance, personal empowerment, spirituality, the Divine masculine.

YOUR NATAL MOON PHASE

Although this book is aimed at enhancing your life through the energy of your Sun sign, a bit of Lunar help can give your wishing a boost! As well as using the planetary days and hours system to add a bit of zest to your wish fulfilment, try combining your Sun sign's power periods with your natal Moon phase (your natal Moon phase can be calculated using a number of sources on the internet, or through an astrologer), or even studying which constellation the Moon is situated in at certain times, to increase the power of your spells and asking rituals. For example, you might like to 'ask' for a promotion at work during a New/Waxing Moon period, particularly if the Moon happens to fall under an auspicious sign for career advancement, such as Capricorn. Your natal Moon phase can also be used to similar effect, by researching when your Moon phase will coincide with a certain Lunar constellation position.

In most astrological interpretations the Sun is regarded as the most important, central feature of a natal chart. But to many the Moon is equally, if not more, important than the Sun sign. Many ancient cultures considered the Moon sign to be more significant. The Moon passes through the 12 signs about every 2.5 days, usually covering the whole zodiac in around 27.3 days. The Moon symbolises our inner world, the world of feeling, emotions, habitual responses, instincts, intuition, security and the subconscious. It describes our nurturing style and needs, our emotional response to life, our attitudes and likely reactions to others, our instinctive and habitual responses, the receptive feminine side of ourselves, our experience of our mother or mother figure, and our childhood experience. It represents the soul. In relationships it symbolises how we like to be nurtured and cared for, and the potential depth of our involvement on personal intimate levels.

For many centuries, people across the world have recognised that the Moon influences the affairs of all living things on planet Earth. The waxing Moon appears to have a drawing, increasing and enhancing effect, whereas the waning Moon has a decreasing, receding and withdrawing effect. All things that come into being are stamped with the qualities of the prevailing Moon stage. It seems that people born during certain Lunar phases tend to share specific attributes with other people born during this same phase. In turn, their attributes will be subtly different from those of individuals born during any of the other stages in the Moon cycle. Knowing exactly which phase of the Moon you were born under gives you all kinds of extraordinarily valuable insights into your character, emotions, behaviour and motivations in life. It can make you aware of your deepest underlying drives, the fundamental purpose that you are drawn towards in life and the contribution you can make to others and society during the course of your lifetime. This knowledge may enable you to intuit and make the most of your own personal cyclical pattern that you go through each month, and allow you to know when the most auspicious periods of time are for you and your affairs, nurture yourself and channel your energies in the most positive directions.

Because this Lunar pattern repeats itself every month, you will find that you can even pace yourself on a long-term basis. This will enable you to effectively target your efforts and goals on periods of time that you know will be potentially fortunate for you. You may in fact find that your birth phase corresponds with the days of the month when you have abundant energy, feel inspired and can generate new ideas with ease. During this period, you should work towards the fruition of your efforts, bring your dreams into light and reach for the stars!

The Lunar Phases Are:

★ New Moon
★ First/Waxing Crescent
★ First Quarter
★ Waxing Gibbous Moon
★ Full Moon
★ Waning Gibbous / Disseminating Moon
★ Last Quarter
★ Waning Crescent / Balsamic Moon
★ Back to the New Moon

SPELLS, MAGIC & WISHING WITH MOON PHASES

Though the Moon has eight astronomical phases, it is the three phases corresponding to maiden, mother and crone that are the most significant in spells, ritual, wish magic and psychic work. By tuning into the physical Moon we can understand and harness these distinct energy phases in our daily lives and magical worlds. The four primary Lunar phases are the New Moon, First Quarter, Full Moon and the Last Quarter. Depending on what sort of spell you wish to perform, your spell should take place during one of these cycles or time periods. Each phase of the Moon is good for some types of magic, but not so much for others.

NEW MOON, WAXING & FIRST QUARTER

In astronomical terms, the New Moon occurs when the Moon rises and sets at the same time as the Sun. Both bodies are found in the same position compared with the Earth. Therefore, a Solar eclipse can only ever occur at the New Moon, when the two luminaries are found, for a short time, in a perfect line relative to the Earth, with the Moon positioned between the Sun and the Earth. The New Moon's sunlit face is hidden from the Earth.

In astrological terms, the New Moon occurs at a time when the Sun and the Moon are found in the same degree of the zodiac and therefore occupy the same zodiac sign, forming a conjunction, or a 'fusing' of energies.

In astronomical terms, the First Quarter occurs seven days after the New Moon. Seen from the Earth, this phase makes the Moon like a crescent, forming the shape of a capital D.

In astrological terms, it occurs when the Sun and the Moon form a ninety-degree angle, or the square aspect, inside the zodiac, the Moon always preceding the Sun.

As the New Moon marks the beginning of a new cycle, it symbolises fresh starts. This is an exceptional time to work magic and make wishes for new beginnings, and for the conception and initiation of new projects. Use this Moon phase for improving health, the gradual increase of prosperity, attracting good luck, fertility magic, finding new love, friendship or romance, job hunting, making plans for the future and increasing your general spiritual or psychic awareness.

Overall, the Waxing Crescent and First Quarter Moon phases are appropriate for spells, rituals and workings that involve growth, healing and increase. This is a period of time lasting approximately two weeks, to draw things toward you and increase things, such as love, prosperity and new opportunities. During this period is the time to bless new projects, anything that requires energy to grow, such as gardens, business ventures, new homes, or educational pursuits. Personal growth and healing are accented, as is 'attraction magic' - drawing something to you such as love, abundance, health, success or a new path - and if done well, you can expect results by the next Full Moon. Magical workings for gain, increase or bringing things to you should be initiated when the Moon is waxing (or New, going from Dark to Full). A time for divination of all kinds, spells of spiritual intention, and for any creative project you wish to see birthed, with magical and fruitful results.

While making a wish within the first forty-eight hours after the New Moon is a powerful way of helping it come to fruition, the most potent time for making wishes is actually within the first eight hours of the exact time of its position. Write down your wish list within this first eight hours on a piece of appropriately coloured paper with a special writing tool, and be sure to capture the essence of your wish by wording it in a way that charges your emotions and simply feels 'right'. Make a maximum of ten wishes (less is perfectly fine too), as making too many wishes might disperse their energy too much to be effective. After writing down your list and releasing your wishes to the Universe in whichever form you feel happy with, keep your list and check on it in a few days', weeks' or months' time to assess whether anything has shifted in the direction of your listed dreams, desires or goals. I'll bet it has - or at the very least, something even better has arrived in its place!

Although the first forty-eight hours after the New Moon is the most potent time to make a special wish, you can begin Waxing Moon magic when you can see the crescent in the sky and continue until the day before the Full Moon. The closer to the Full Moon, the more intense the energies. In fact, a personally devised ritual using any special Lunar-associated materials over three days up to and including the Full Moon is excellent for something you require urgently or within a short timeframe.

In some cultures, people turn over silver coins or jewellery three times when the crescent Moon appears in the sky and make a wish. As the Moon grows, it is believed that prosperity and good fortune will grow too.

While the New Moon is not known as a time for 'banishing' or releasing things we no longer want in our lives, I feel that if we are to ask and wish for things, we need to make room to receive them. Making room means that the Universe can slot it right into our lives where we have cleared our paths for it. Clutter, unwanted things, unhappy relationships, possessions that no longer serve us, are all things we can banish. So, to help what you are asking for come into your life quicker, the New Moon is a particularly opportune time to throw a few things out so you can make way for the new and clear up some space for that which you are wishing for. What are you waiting for? Start creating a space for your wishes today!

FULL MOON

In astronomical terms, the Full Moon occurs 14 days after the New Moon, on the day when the Moon sets at the same time the Sun rises, or conversely. The two luminaries are effectively facing each other, with the Earth in between, the Sun shining its light onto the reflective Moon, giving it the fully lit up appearance of a giant, bright, perfectly round sphere. Indeed, its entire face is bathed in sunlight. A Lunar eclipse can only occur at the Full Moon, when the Sun, Moon and Earth are all in line, and the Earth hides the lit side of the Moon to us.

In astrological terms, a Full Moon occurs at the time when the Sun and Moon are 180 degrees apart inside the zodiac, and therefore positioned in opposite signs, forming an opposition aspect.

The highest energy occurs at the Full Moon, making this is a powerful time for all manner of magical workings. Use the Full Moon phase for any immediate need, a sudden boost of power or courage, psychic protection, a change of career or location, travel, healing acute health conditions, the consummation of love or a commitment, justice, ambition and promotion of all kinds. This phase lasts approximately 3 days - 24 hours before the exact Full Moon, the day of, and 24 hours after it, according to many sources - giving us 3 full days to perform our spells. However, we are not strictly limited to a three-day period; the power of this phase can actually be accessed for seven days - three days prior to, the night of, and the three days after the Full Moon. The Full Moon period is when the Moon is at her most powerful, being the most luminous and radiant part of the cycle. Known as the 'high tide' of psychic power, the Full Moon represents culmination, climax, fulfilment and abundance. The Full Moon governs all kinds of magic, including manifestation, banishing, and is particularly good for calling forth protection and heightening your intuitive abilities. The Full Moon contains magic that calls forth personal power, fertility, spiritual development, and psychic awareness. Cleansing of ritual tools, crystals, wish lists, Tarot decks, and the like can be done during this phase. Magic worked during the Full Moon often takes one complete cycle to come to fruition. Try also reaffirming your desires during the New Moon to give them an added nudge in the right direction.

LAST QUARTER OR WANING MOON

In astronomical terms, the Last Quarter, or Waning Moon, occurs twenty-one days after the New Moon. The time difference between the rising and setting of the two luminaries is reduced to what it was at the First Quarter. Viewed from the Earth, the Moon resembles a crescent whose lit up area is decreasing in size, forming the shape of a capital C.

In astrological terms, the Waning Moon occurs when the Sun and Moon are positioned at ninety degree angles of each other in the zodiac, forming the square aspect again. However, during this phase, the Sun is instead *ahead* of the Moon.

The Waning Moon represents the Lunar cycle from Full to Dark. Any spells and magic performed during this period is based purely around banishing and releasing. It could involve releasing things which no longer serve you (such as behaviours, material things, relationships and attitudes), banishing negative energies, and removing obstacles which are standing in the way of achieving your goals or dreams. The Waning Moon is the best time for cleansing, gently releasing, eliminating, expelling and completion. It is of great assistance when you are wanting to let go of something, or someone, gradually. The Dark of the Moon, the period when the Moon is no longer visible to the naked eye, until the New Moon, is the most useful time for divination of all kinds.

★ What is your natal Moon phase type?
Can you think of ways you can combine it with the power of your Sun sign to effect change and bring about wonderful happenings? ★

HARNESSING YOUR PERSONAL MOON MAGIC ★ MOON IN ARIES

When the Moon is in your sign of Aries, it is a great time for working magic around: Your inner warrior, personal power, innovation, strengthening your confidence, force, expression, self-preservation under threat, fearlessness, self-reliance, independence, spontaneity, enthusiasm, optimism and hope, and assertiveness. Suggested operations could be around rituals and spells for learning new things, gaining confidence, taking initiative in a situation, sporting prowess and success, starting a new project, winning, controlling fear or anger, making announcements, being a pioneer, tapping into personal originality and new frontiers, taking calculated risks and boosting motivation. It is also an opportune time to call forth a stronger sense of Self and ego. With the Moon in Aries, all situations relating to new beginnings, new projects, and opportunities for self-improvement are enhanced.

THE MOON ★ WHAT IT REPRESENTS IN THE HUMAN PSYCHE & NATAL CHART

The Moon in the sky shines with the reflected light of the Sun. Although not a planet, the Moon is our nearest celestial neighbour and exerts a great influence upon us. The gravitational pull of the Moon affects our body fluids, which contribute to about 90 per cent of our biological make-up. It moves at approximately half a degree per hour and takes an average of 27.3 days to pass through all twelve zodiac signs, staying in each for around 2.5 days.

In astrology the Moon corresponds with the way in which we reflect and respond to what is going on around us. It has to do with our feelings, emotions and instincts and, in the same way the Moon influences the tides on planet Earth, it symbolises the ebb and flow of our emotional nature, our moods, fluctuations and changeability. The Moon is the archetype of the Mother, which is within us all, and represents the primary feminine principle in the natal chart. It is through the Moon that we express our parental instincts - caring, nurturing, protecting, sensitivity. The Moon has links with the past and the subconscious and it is from this almost primitive source that our natural instinctual forces flow.

The Moon is essentially a feminine principle and associates with the inner personality, receptivity, passivity and inward-oriented feelings. It can act as an inner guide to the deeper self, the unconscious self, figures half-shrouded in mystery, linking the hidden personal world of the subconscious to the clearer world of personal awareness.

The Moon is the innermost core of our being, private feelings, habitual reactions and subconscious habits. It is the caring, nurturing sustainer of life, the 'mother' of the zodiac. It tells us about how we seek security, our urge to nurture, our nurturing style, our responses and feelings and moods. The innermost core of our being, private feelings, subconscious habits. It is concerned with habits, mothering, habitual/instinctive responses and personality. It is our karma, our soul, our past.

The Moon represents our mother or mother figure, our feminine side, maternal instinct, our nurturing style and needs, our unconscious self, our emotional reactions, the subconscious, our feelings, instincts, intuition, receptivity, habits, what we need to feel secure, fluctuations, cycles, moods, and our childhood. Its position in the birth chart is very significant, because as well as revealing feminine qualities and the potential gentleness and tenderness of a being, the Moon also reveals important information about the experiences and expression of the five senses

The Moon is essentially receptive and passive; it reflects the life experience rather than initiating it. Fluctuating and cyclical, the Moon is the planet (although technically a satellite) of the childhood experience, and instinctual reactions. It represents the mother (a child's experience and expectations of their mother), maternal instincts and the feminine principle, indicating how strongly these manifest in an individual, male or female. As it represents what our childhood experience is likely to be, and childhood is essentially a time where our consciousness has not yet fully developed, our Moon sign traits seem to be more apparent in our younger years. We will usually show our Moon sign traits more so than our Sun sign traits during this developing period of infancy and early childhood, until we have the presence of mind to more consciously develop our ego and true core Self (the Sun).

The symbol for the Moon ☽ is a representation of its crescent in its waxing phase from new to full, but it can also be seen as two half circles - these form a bowl shape, a receptacle, a feminine container that 'receives' and 'holds' anything put into it. The half circle, unlike the full circle of the Sun, is finite and incomplete, almost as if striving for wholeness.

The Moon represents our *soul*.

YOUR MOON SIGN

The Sun / Moon Polarity
Conscious & Unconscious, Night & Day, Yin & Yang

"Man does, woman is."
Edward Edinger

Your Moon Sign, representing your soul, and your Sun sign, representing your spirit, work together to form the foundation of your basic personality, expression and nature. If you know what your Moon sign is, look it up below and read how it works with your Arien Sun to blend your mind, soul and spirit.

♈ **With the Moon in ARIES, Sun in Aries,** you are likely to be ★ Self-centred, heroic, passionate, optimistic, egocentric, courageous, quick-thinking, bold, innovatively minded, on the go, impatient, active, blunt, self-interested, progressive, alert, childish, impetuous, enthusiastic, independent, honest, adventurous, hot-tempered, assertive, insensitive, ambitious, youthful, self-reliant, energetic, bossy, emotionally reckless, restless, speak before thinking, a fast communicator, pioneering, original, blunt, forward-looking, lively, witty, frank, bright, an individualist, and possess a touchy ego and personal integrity, as well as a maverick with a crusading temperament.

Sun/Moon Harmony Rating ★ *7.5 out of 10*

♉ **With the Moon in TAURUS, Sun in Aries,** you are likely to be ★ Possessive, stubborn, persistent, jealous, materialistic, conflicted between security and freedom, sexy, tenacious, physically and mentally robust, devoted, powerfully charming, pushy, loyal, reluctant to listen to others' views if convinced your own are correct, stoic, faithful, bossy, friendly, capable, determined, resourceful, enthusiastic about making money, an entrepreneur, ambitious, strong-willed, reliable, philanthropic, in possession of a bawdy sense of humour and strong sense of self, and dedicated to activating your inspired ideas in the real, material world.

Sun/Moon Harmony Rating ★ *5 out of 10*

♊ **With the Moon in GEMINI, Sun in Aries,** you are likely to be ★ Sociable, persuasive, deft, charming, a free spirit, changeable, friendly, bright, breezy, emotionally versatile, quick-witted, flippant, vital, perceptive, clever, inspiring, stimulating, flexible, adaptable, curious, childlike, emotionally impulsive, vivacious, zany, inconsistent, expressive, restless, easily bored, active, inspired, a live wire, direct, humorous, funny, creative, progressive, communicative, strongly socially aware, unsentimental, emotionally naïve, gifted, a wonderful friend, unreliable, zestful, an opportunist, original, popular, funny, easily swept away by ideas and concepts, open towards and perceptive of new ideas, pioneering, idealistic, intellectual, fun-loving, squandering of your natural talents, reluctant to delve deeper into anything, on the go, inquisitive, too busy to deal with feelings, have too many irons in the fire, and in possession of the gift of the gab and a sunny, breezy and light-hearted disposition.

Sun/Moon Harmony Rating ★ *8.5 out of 10*

♋ **With the Moon in CANCER, Sun in Aries,** you are likely to be ★ Temperamental, sensitive, inspiring, clannish, devoted, romantic, affectionate, demonstrative, inspired to help others, unstable, inconsistent, torn between the past and future, feeling, richly imaginative, indirectly self-assertive, initiating, volatile, uplifting to others, intuitive, emotionally expressive, socially conscious, passionate about family, compassionate, a kind-hearted rebel, generous, imaginative, creative, kind, devoted to the triumph of the human spirit through action, helpful, companionable, a sensitive individualist, self-reliant, a good leader, emotionally defensive, and occasionally moved to emotional outbursts which may undermine your greatest talents and achievements.

Sun/Moon Harmony Rating ★ *7 out of 10*

♌ **With the Moon in LEO, Sun in Aries,** you are likely to be ★ Proud, independent, warm-hearted, individualistic, strong-willed, dramatic, fearless, bold, artistic, generous to a fault, original, charismatic, passionate, radiant, zestful, vital, uplifting, immediate, sulky, childish, demanding, enthusiastic, active, adventurous, vain, friendly, a good leader, enthusiastically romantic, explorative, imaginative, open, powerful, extroverted, self-interested, honest, inclined to get carried away by drama and fun, idealistic, egotistical, direct, controlling, bossy, expressive, ambitious, despotic, self-centred, creative, emotionally radiating of warmth, luxury-loving, helpful, demonstrative, creatively imaginative, optimistic, impatient, sociable, playful, larger than life, intensely devoted, heroic, honourable, a big thinker, and able to inspire others with your large appetite for life.

Sun/Moon Harmony Rating ★ *8 out of 10* **

♍ **With the Moon in VIRGO, Sun in Aries,** you are likely to be ★ Intelligent, selfish yet dutiful, judgemental, clever, discriminating, perfectionist, striving, methodical, studious, an avid researcher, outspoken yet reserved, bossy yet diffident, willing to put your cards on the table and say what you think, helpful, serious, kind-hearted, caring, innovative, mentally alert, mentally dextrous, efficient, reserved, straightforward, adaptable, quietly passionate, intolerant of others' weaknesses, analytical, critical, outrageous but often conventional, willing to help and do what needs to be done, altruistic, conscientious, effective, disciplined, genuinely kind, bright, devoted to ideals, dry-witted, zestful yet uptight, and in possession of a dedicated loyalty, with a strong craftsmanship streak.

Sun/Moon Harmony Rating ★ *6 out of 10*

♎ **With the Moon in LIBRA, Sun in Aries,** you are likely to be ★ Lively, intellectually precocious, gregarious, see life from endlessly new vantage points, sociable, refined, easy going, affectionate, forthright, confident but indecisive, convivial, amorous, popular, emotionally expressive, charming, approachable, spirited, courteous, eager for life, tolerant, ingenious, chivalrous, accessible, civilised, sharing, approval-seeking, hospitable, hedonistic, interested in others, romantically idealistic, endearing, loving of people, colourfully persuasive, procrastinating, outgoing, artistic, creative, gracefully enthusiastic, self-centred but kind, flirtatious, inspiring, hopeful, vain, considerate, thoughtful, emotionally naïve, courageous but strategic, a maverick but a seeker of justice, vacillating between one's own needs and the needs of other people, and conflicted between independence and needing others.

Sun/Moon Harmony Rating ★ *8.5 out of 10*

♏ **With the Moon in SCORPIO, Sun in Aries,** you are likely to be ★ Intense, magnetic, highly motivated, self-dramatising, powerful, forceful, ambitious, highly charged, extreme, active, aggressively optimistic, determined, undeterred, pushy, possessive, keenly insightful, investigative, unbending, narcissistic, insatiable, strong-willed, dominating, intensely dedicated, passionate, unyielding, purposeful, sharp, highly sexed, overbearing, difficult, resourceful, extremely resilient, controlling, persuasive, charismatic, stubborn, persevering and thorough, devoted to truth at any cost, fiercely independent, penetrative, loyal, emotional, courageously dedicated, compulsive, perceptive, self-reliant, stern, exacting, potentially ruthless and manipulative, emotionally powerful, in possession of an unshakeable belief in yourself and others' individual worth, as well as a strong sense of self and personal integrity.

Sun/Moon Harmony Rating ★ *6.5 out of 10*

♐ **With the Moon in SAGITTARIUS, Sun in Aries,** you are likely to be ★ Frank, tolerant, talkative, eager, impatient, friendly, feisty, independent, idealistic, explorative, an avid traveller, big-hearted, honest, adventurous, impatient with petty details and restrictions, visionary, confident, competitive, outspoken, big-hearted, highly strung, emphatic, prone to preach or boss others around, brash, loving of a challenge, insensitive, self-absorbed, grandiose, a daredevil, rash, inquisitive, self-assured, zestful, distant from your feelings, emotionally reckless, a free spirit, in possession of a keen sense of humour, egocentric, extravagant, careless, contagiously optimistic, inspiring, outrageous, aspiring, gregarious, trusting, naïve, expansive, verbose, philosophical, freedom-seeking, morally certain, residing in the realm of limitless possibilities and guided by your inner fire rather than emotion.

Sun/Moon Harmony Rating ★ *8.5 out of 10* **

♑ **With the Moon in CAPRICORN, Sun in Aries,** you are likely to be ★ Steadfast, realistic, tough-minded, forceful, authoritarian, persistent, aggressive, ardent, the boss, the winner, resourceful, enterprising, entrepreneurial, a natural leader, astute, no-nonsense, blunt, controlling, overpowering, committed, independent, driven to succeed, ambitious, critical, cool, unstoppable, unemotional, wise, shrewd, organised, efficient, serious, sensible, materialistic, understanding of practical applications and wisdom, economical, a good leader, personally honourable, strict on self, fearless, uptight, self-contained, sardonically humorous, willing to work hard, and in possession of an overall attitude of 'shoot for the stars' (while keeping your feet firmly on the ground at the same time).

Sun/Moon Harmony Rating ★ *7 out of 10*

♒ **With the Moon in AQUARIUS, Sun in Aries,** you are likely to be ★ Frank, sharp, selfish yet altruistic, intriguing, a people person, incisive, full of bright ideas, congenial, torn between Self and others, friendly, tolerant, independent, extraverted, idealistic, emotionally detached, eccentric, 'different', unconventional, revolutionary, a social activist, aloof, paradoxical, imaginative, sympathetic, unconventional, honest, original, forward-moving, inventive, impersonal in relationships, clear-headed, charismatic, a social visionary, impatient with practical details, highly observant, acutely aware of the human condition, progressive, scientifically oriented, objective, living an unusual lifestyle in some way, well-meaning, dramatic, open to the unusual, emotionally naïve, over-identifying with causes, blunt and insensitive when comparing people with your ideals, freedom-loving, unorthodox, idealistic, impractical, loyal, exceptionally individual, humanitarian, globally aware, courageous and committed to your ideals, a law unto yourself, in possession of an eternal sense of hope and belief in others, and making friends right across the fascinating broad spectrum of human viewpoints.

Sun/Moon Harmony Rating ★ *8 out of 10*

♓ **With the Moon in PISCES, Sun in Aries,** you are likely to be ★ Imaginative, loving, giving, intuitive, enthusiastically mystical, idealistic, trusting, a chaser of spiritual rainbows, vulnerable, open, receptive, procrastinating, uncertain, self-doubting, weak-willed, good-natured, intriguing, kindly, friendly, emotionally aware, sentimental, single-minded but dreamy, impulsive, careless, accepting, understanding, independent but vulnerable, a zestful poet, altruistic, visionary, insightful, generous, receptive, creative, reverent, forgiving, devoted, mysterious, paradoxical, empathetic, impressionable, naïve, innocent, easily swayed, gullible, impractical, evasive, perceptive, emotionally intelligent, able to adapt to any situation, romantic, emotionally expressive, dramatic, restless, a worrier, temperamental, hopeful, able to mix and work with all types of people, aware of the needs of others, and in possession of a wonderfully offbeat but original philosophy of life.

Sun/Moon Harmony Rating ★ *7.5 out of 10*

** If your Moon is in Leo or Sagittarius, your Sun and Moon will form what is known in astrology as a trine aspect. This aspect is the easiest, most flowing and harmonious astrological aspect, ensuring that your Sun and Moon, or spirit and soul, are well integrated. With both luminaries in Fire signs, this gives them the best possible degree of complementary energy - a blending of the elements suggests a balanced expression of personality. One drawback of the trine aspect lies in the fact that its easy flow can be *too* harmonious; if our path is too smooth and difficulties don't arise to challenge us from time to time, we can often become lazy and complacent, stunting our growth and spiritual evolution. As Fire signs, you share the art of vitality, zest, enthusiasm, broad-mindedness, affability, idealism, independence, drive, ambition, force, affection, warm-heartedness, generosity, sociability, and have extravagant tastes, but may be temperamental, dramatic, overbearing, egocentric, restless, bossy, insensitive, careless, arrogant and self-centred.

YOUR BODY & HEALTH

"A physician without a knowledge of astrology has no right to call himself a physician."
Hippocrates (born c. 460 BC)

Hippocrates, the fifth century BC Greek physician and 'father of medicine' and supposed author of the Hippocratic Oath, maintained that no one should be allowed to practise medicine who had not first studied astrology. Another Greek physician, Claudius Galen, brought together a huge range of knowledge and ideas in the second century AD which dominated medical practice until the 17th century. Among his teachings was a diagnostic technique which assumed that illnesses and their treatments were affected by and governed by the phases of the Moon. For centuries, astrology was a compulsory component of medical training (and still is in some natural medicine degrees), albeit only one aspect of diagnosis and treatment.

Medical or health astrology concerns particular ways of determining and interpreting an individual's horoscope with particular reference to health issues - diagnosis of current dis-eases, identification of areas of bodily weaknesses, and the prescription of natural cures and remedies. In ancient times, and still even today, the movement of the stars and planets was believed to affect bodily functions, and to cause ailments, or cure them.

During the Middle Ages, many drawings of the 'zodiac man' were made, which showed which signs of the zodiac were related to each part of the body, providing information as to the best times of the year to undertake cures for ailments affecting the corresponding body parts.

Health astrology persists today in many forms and among astrologers themselves, from whom clients seek counsel on health-related issues, and while it certainly cannot be used diagnose a condition or dis-ease, one's Sun sign, along with other factors of the natal chart, can definitely indicate potential problem areas of weakness or possible troubles. This branch of astrology has been found to be surprisingly accurate in most cases. While mostly accurate, none of the following information should ever be used as a substitute for professional medical advice should you be personally concerned about any of the conditions or afflictions listed for your Sun sign.

ARIEN HEALTH

Aries is associated with the Head (particularly the Cerebrum, where the upper brain lies), Skull, Face, Brain, Sinuses, Pituitary Gland, the Muscular System, the Adrenals, Blood Pressure, and the Left Cerebellum and the Frontal Lobe areas of the brain. Fevers and accidents are typical of all Fire signs, especially the highly-strung and risk-taking Aries, but recovery is usually rapid and achieved through willpower and an underlying basis of physical fortitude. Burns, injuries from sharp objects, and head injuries are common, and you are the most vulnerable of the zodiac to these, so care is needed to curb any tendencies which may place you at risk of these. Some other ailments Aries may suffer from are epilepsy, neuralgia, migraines, brain inflammations, hay fever, dizziness, nose bleeds, high blood pressure, acne, sinuses, upper jaw conditions, toothaches, ear and eye complaints, and headaches. You may also encounter difficulties with the cerebrum and carotid arteries, as these too are Aries-ruled areas. The head is particularly vulnerable in your sign, and knocks and bumps to this region are common in Arien children, prompting an early visit by the Tooth Fairy.

Yours is one of the healthiest signs of the zodiac. You are bursting with reserves of energy and have great recuperative powers, but you can burn yourself to a temporary standstill more easily than most too. Your constitution is built for spontaneous, intense, short bursts of exertion, and you can endanger your health when you work strenuously for long periods, as endurance is not your forte. Your nature is to be constantly up and doing, both physically and mentally, and any threat to this mobility would mortify you. If you do become immobilised for any period of time, you become quite indignant about it.

Every Arien, at some stage in his life, will indulge in rash behaviour that brings an injury to the head or face. And although you can survive head fevers strong enough to kill the average mortal, your headstrong Martian tendency to carry on regardless can be to your detriment. The root cause of most head conditions such as headaches and migraines, can usually be attributed to anger, stress, frustration and impatience. Cuts and burns are also likely. Skin rashes, peptic ulcers, high blood pressure, kneecap injury, stomach ailments and all acute illnesses may also plague you.

Haemorrhages through accidents are a danger. Because of your incessant haste, you are often tripping and colliding with things. This, combined with your love of sports, speed and the outdoor life, means the risk of injuries such as bruises and cuts are considerable. Not many Ariens are without at least one significant scar on their bodies.

Despite your usually robust health, you are particularly vulnerable to drafts and dampness. You suffer quite often from head colds, which may develop into sinus infections, ear complaints and nagging headaches. Neuralgia is a common complaint, as is arthritis, particularly of the hands.

Ariens seldom suffer from drawn-out chronic illness; should you acquire a disease, your decline or demise is likely to be just as rapid as its onset, although you do make quick recoveries. Such is your fear of being ill or struck down that you don't like visiting the doctor, and will try as many 'self-treatment' methods as possible first. At the root of your dislike of doctors is your fear of being told the truth about the seriousness of an illness or condition; you would rather press on, hoping it will go away.

Ariens need abundant exercise to keep their systems in good working order. Exercise is important for everyone of course, but for Ariens it is vital to their wellbeing and effective functioning. You may well be so enthusiastic that you overdo physical regimes or sporting pursuits, and moderation may be needed if excessive strain or injury is to be avoided. Learning to avoid overdoing things in general, both mentally and physically, will keep you healthy. Ariens need to slow down and rest regularly.

Your ruling planet Mars is traditionally associated with the Left Ear, Kidneys, Veins, Blood, Iron, Motor Nerves, and rules the Gonads (sex glands) and the Genitals. As well, it governs the Forehead, Bile, Nose, Gall Bladder, Penis, Left Hemisphere of the Brain, and the Muscular System. Other Mars-influenced health concerns may involve the muscles, head, adrenal glands, inflammations, red blood corpuscles, and energy levels

Overall, the Ram represents activation of energy. Aries's nature is hot, dry and inflammatory. Your childlike approach to life can lead to accidents and injuries and you are prone to overtaxing your systems and dissipating your vital force. Keeping yourself in excellent health overall, with a special awareness of Aries' vulnerable points, is key to achieving all you set out to do, and getting the most out of your life!

THE CELL SALTS ★ ASTROLOGICAL TONICS

Homeopathy and astrology have colluded to provide a wonderful list of astrological tonics, one particularly suited to each of the twelve signs. These are called 'homeopathic cell salts', 'tissue salts' or 'biochemic cell salts', and are available in most health food stores, are inexpensive and easy to take. They are considered to be gentle, effective and safe, even for children, people in fragile health states, and the elderly. Although the full picture, drawn from a full natal horoscope, gives a fuller, more accurate idea of an individual's unique constitution, even simply working with one's date of birth can be enough for the medical astrologer to suggest the use of a cell salt based upon the correlation with an individual's Sun sign.

As well as the cell salts having a significant effect upon physical ailments, they can also profoundly influence the subtle energy bodies, including the mental, emotional, etheric and spiritual. Although the most common use of these salts is based upon each salt's correspondence with a Sun sign, use of the cell salt related to one's Moon sign can assist with addressing deeper underlying emotional issues, such as anxiety, depression, panic and fear. Use of the cell salt relating to your Moon sign will therefore help to restore your sense of safety, balance, security and emotional resilience. In the first seven years of life, when the Moon is the most influential sphere in our lives, Lunar cell salts are the most appropriate choice as a remedy or tonic.

For specific health problems, take both the salt of your Sun or Moon sign, *and* the salt that pertains to the specific condition. The same principle applies to the Ascendant sign, as the First House represents one's physical health, and especially if the Sun or Moon is a rising planet, which means rulership of the whole chart. For the purposes of this book, however, the cell salt that correlates with your Sun sign only is outlined.

TISSUE SALT FOR ARIES ★ KALI PHOS.

Kalium Phosphate, or Kali Phos. (Potassium phosphate) is the cell salt for Aries. As Aries governs the head and muscle tissue, this cell salt is needed to help repair nerves, muscles and grey matter. Potassium phosphate is found in all fluids and tissues of the body, especially the nerve cells, grey matter, plasma, muscles and blood cells. The exchange of gases in respiration and breakdown of fatty tissue depends upon this salt, as do all oxidation processes. Hindering decay in an organism, it is nature's great 'antiseptic'. Useful for remedying offensive secretions and excretions, a deficiency of Kali Phos. is often characterised by intense body odour. It is also a nerve nutrient, with a significant effect upon the nerve cells, especially the brain cells. Used for all forms of mental fatigue and its offshoots, Kali Phos. is beneficial for insomnia, dizziness, depression, neuralgia, irritability, hysteria, headaches, and all types of nervous disorders, especially those arising from long hours of concentration or overwork. Kali Phos. helps to create the grey matter of the brain, and Ariens are particularly responsive to this cell salt as Aries rules the external, internal and structural components of the head and brain. Foods rich in this tissue salt include dandelion, potato skin, cabbage, milk, asparagus, beetroot, dates, cucumber, asparagus, lettuce, tomato, apple, lemon, celery, grapefruit, cauliflower, watercress, orange, parsley, carrot and spinach.

FIRE SIGN ARIES & THE CHOLERIC HUMOUR

Greek physician Hippocrates (460 - 370 BC) theorised that certain human behaviours were caused by body fluids, called 'humours'. Later, Galen of Pergamon (AD 131 - 200), a Greek physician, developed the first typology of temperaments to encompass many facets of the human psyche and physiology. These also related to the classical elements of Fire, Earth, Air and Water - as choleric, melancholic, sanguine and phlegmatic respectively. According to the Greeks who developed the temperament theory (the word stems from the Latin word *temperamentum*, meaning mixture), temperament is the 'mixture' of qualities that combine to form elements in physics and humours in medicine. The Greeks sought equilibrium in the four qualities of hot, cold, wet (moist), and dry, the elements of Earth, Air, Fire and Water, and the four humours of choler or yellow bile, melancholer or black bile, blood and phlegm. If balance was achieved, the person was said to be well- or even-tempered, and the importance of determining the temperament allowed for imbalances to be treated.

In ancient times, each of the four types of humours corresponded to a different personality type, which were associated with a domination of various biological functions. It was suggested that the temperaments came to clearest manifestation in childhood, between around the ages of six and fourteen of age, after which they become subordinate, but still influential, factors in our personality. It is important to note that your temperament is not your personality. However, your personality can incorporate parts of the temperament in its expression. Personality is shaped by both external and internal factors, whereas the temperament is innate, an inborn, inherent part of each individual.

The Fire element corresponds with the humour choleric, which is characterised by a short response time-delay, but response sustained for a relatively long time. Driven by their goals, for which they will use others as tools to achieve them, a choleric disposition represents touchiness, restlessness, aggression, spirit, excitement, changeability, impulsiveness, activity and optimism.

A person with a choleric temperament is one who is strong, wilful and even aggressive if necessary. Impatience and anxiety are features, and physically these traits can elicit a response from the liver - stronger than usual biliary secretions.

The choleric character is associated with Fire, which is the ruling element of summer, the season with which the person under this influence has the greatest affinity. The Martian and Sun types, referring to Mars in Aries and the Sun in Leo, are the most common types amongst the cholerics.

Choleric is associated with the ego level of self. Its taste is salty and sour, its nature acidic, its indication yellow bile. The choleric humour is associated with the astral body ^ *, and with hot and dry conditions.

^ A couple of thousand years ago, the Mesopotamians, Chinese and Egyptians, and more recently the Arabs, practised a medicine called 'of three bodies'. According to the doctors of the ancient world (who often practised as astrologers as well), a human being had three bodies: the physical body, the ethereal (or vital) body and the astral body, imparting a holistic approach to health. In modern medicine, usually only the physical body is focused upon fully. According to tradition, this physical body comprises three principles or states corresponding to three primordial elements: *solid* (Earth), *liquid* (Water) and *gas* (Air). This is the material body, the physical outer cover of muscles, nerves and organs held together by the skeleton. The Fire element corresponds with the *astral* body, which sits outside the physical body in one's auric field.

* The primordial element linked to the astral body is Fire, and it includes seven points, or doors, of perception which correspond exactly with the chakras. The astral body has a degree of vibration and radiance which is far higher than that of the ethereal body, an area which sits just beyond the physical body in one's auric field. Ancient physicians believed that this radiance covered an area varying from 40 centimetres to three metres around the physical body, and that this area varied greatly depending on the psychic energy of the individual. (The higher the levels, the larger the area of the radiance). The astral body is described as a diffused outer layer with whirls and flashing swirls of colour which move constantly. The intensity of its colour and movement varies according to the pattern of thoughts, feelings, emotions, moods and desires of the individual.

MONEY ATTRIBUTES

Colour for Increased Earning Power ★ Red

The following plants can be used by all zodiac signs to assist in attracting money ★ Ginger, Allspice, Clover, Orange, Marjoram, Cinnamon, Sassafras, Woodruff, Bergamot, Tonka Beans, Heliotrope, Alfalfa, Coltsfoot, Thyme, Mace, Irish Moss, Clove, Almond, Corn, Honeysuckle, Sesame, Nutmeg, Vetiver, Poppy, Jasmine, Dill and Elder Flower. To attract luck and success, try using any of the above, combined with any of the following: Alfalfa Seeds, Basil, Mustard Seeds, Vervain Leaves, Poppy Seeds, Rosemary, Lemon, Anise and Holly.

Striving for financial gain and abundance with a healthy inner moral compass is, in my view, one of the most noble goals we can set for ourselves. When we have more money, we are better placed to help ourselves and of course others; after all, as Abraham Maslow's Hierarchy of Needs model (1943) attests, once our primary and base survival needs have been satisfied, we can then advance higher towards loftier achievements, such as self-confidence, creativity and self-actualisation. Prosperity allows us to turn our attention to these more transcendental matters - to reach for lives not just of material comfort and luxuries, but of meaning, generosity, balance, harmony, fulfilment and joy. Our Sun sign can offer clues as to how we go about acquiring, earning, saving, maintaining, and allowing the overall flow of giving and receiving money. What's *your* money style?

> "It doesn't seem to break the Mars spirit that cash doesn't always cling to him, perhaps because what he seeks is not necessarily in the bank."
> **Linda Goodman**

As suggested by Linda Goodman's quote above, Aries is essentially an idealist when it comes to money and what it can buy. "Give him a choice of money or glory, and he'll take glory any time," she goes on to add on the Aries spirit when it comes to financial matters. Conquering and striving is what Aries is all about, and whether he has one dollar in the bank or one million, he will feel rich just for having run - and won - the race to attain it.

Aries are likely to make money from entrepreneurial enterprises but need to watch out for impulsive decisions and the need for instant gratification and quick returns. You spend freely and on a whim, with a penchant for risk-taking, and are rarely tempted by safeguards such as insurance and savings plans. Aries enjoys the thrill of gambling, and any speculative spending is usually done so only if there is opportunity to make money swiftly and easily.

Money is important to you, mainly because of the things it can buy, and being impetuous and rather childlike, you tend to spend lavishly and thoughtlessly. Usually willing to save up for certain things, you are often lucky in that money comes to you freely. You tend to have a knack for keeping the money flowing in, but it can sometimes flow out again just as easily! On top of this, you are incredibly generous, but need to keep this in check if you give too freely on too regular a basis. You are forever trying to widen your financial horizons in whatever means possible. Being an independent spirit and a bit of a freedom-seeker, you love that money can indeed buy you the lifestyle you desire - and that, to you, is the ultimate freedom.

COLOURS

Chromatomancy, or divination by colour, is a form of energy therapy that has been used for thousands of years by many different cultures. It works on the principle that we make both instinctive and rational choices or preferences based on circumstances which are already present in ourselves; colour also has an effect on the energy in an environment, and we in turn respond consciously or subconsciously to our surroundings. If we look at the causes, and try to understand the reasons, as to why we are so receptive to one particular colour over another, we will see that there is a subtle link between certain hues and our emotional and instinctive individual reactions. The colour which we give to things results from a combination of three elements:

1. The light or the vibration of a body;

2. The context in which it is found and the interaction between its own light and that of its environment;

3. The sensitivity of the eye's retina which sees the body in question. Because of this, a colour can vary, depending on the individual's perceptions, namely, his sensitivity, his mood, and his view of reality. For a long time, people have understood that their vision of reality depends a lot on their moods, feelings and emotions.

Chromatotherapy, or colour healing, stems from this body of evidence, and its main application is the use of colours for healing purposes. Colours are generally associated with characteristics, feelings, stones, metals, plants and flowers, planets and even the zodiac signs. In varying cultures, they play a significant role in ceremonies and regalia.

We vibrate to the frequency of colour, shown through its continual movement and change in our aura ^. One of the most beautiful examples of colour is the rainbow. This architect of colour is caused by the refraction and internal reflection of light in raindrops. Colour can be perceived as either a pigment, or as illumination. The colour spectrum can be divided into eight main colours: red, orange, yellow, green, turquoise, blue, violet and magenta. Each colour has a wavelength and frequency that carry different therapeutic qualities which have indirect effects upon our health and bodily systems, and because of this, coupled with the fact that we as living energy centres emanate colour, colour can be a great medium in healing, calming, energising, increasing and attracting.

Aristotle, in the fourth century BCE, considered blue and yellow to be the true primary colours and related them to life's polarities: Sun and Moon, male and female, stimulation and sedation, in and out, expansion and contraction. He also associated colours with the four elements of Fire, Earth, Air and Water. Hippocrates, the father of medicine, used colour extensively in medicinal healing and recognised that the therapeutic effects of a white violet differed from those of a purple one. In the fifteenth century, Paracelsus placed particular importance on the role of colour in healing.

Each Sun sign and planetary body has a specific colour or colours which when used in combination with wishing rituals, can enhance their power immensely. Coloured candles can be used to good effect, as the fire energy of the flame/s increases the power of any wish, and flames are also a useful aid to meditating on, focusing upon or clarifying what you want. Coloured candles help to focus the energy for whatever purpose the colour is in sympathy with (e.g. green for money, pink for romance, orange for joy, etc.)

With all this in mind, wearing or using your Sun sign or ruling planet's magical colour/s on a regular basis will undoubtedly bring great benefits.

^ The aura is defined as an energy field, which interpenetrates with, and radiates beyond, the physical body. Clairvoyantly seen, the aura is full of light, colour and shade. The trained healer or seer sees or senses indications within the aura as to the spiritual, physical and emotional state of the individual. Much of the auric colour and energy emanates from the chakras.

YOUR LUCKY COLOURS

For Aries ★ Red, Orange and Yellow - the brighter, the better! Autumnal colours, and white are also fortunate, but should be worn accompanied by other colours.

For Mars ★ Red

Ruled by Mars, the dynamic and headstrong personality of your Fire-inspired sign takes ownership of the colour red. Wearing this colour emphasises Aries' outgoing and commanding nature.

Each of the eight colours of the rainbow spectrum also has a complementary colour to which it is matched. Red is complementary to turquoise, orange to blue, yellow to violet, and green to magenta. If these colour pairs enhance each other's most spellbinding qualities and energies, perhaps you could try wearing your Sun sign's lucky colour with its matching complementary colour in order to produce extra magical results! Your lucky Arien colours are red, which complements turquoise, and orange, which complements blue. Now you know your colours, you can dress for success!

FEATURE COLOURS ★ RED & ORANGE

★ RED ★

Planetary Association ★ Mars

Complementary Colour ★ Turquoise

Healing Qualities ★ Passion, Energy, Confidence, Courage, Sensuality, Security, Power, Inspiration, Activity, Motivation, Dynamism

Keywords ★ Fire, Passion, Aggression, Danger, Power, Desire, Lust, Stop (sign), Strength, Sexual Energy, Courage, Success, Willpower, War, Warning

Red is the colour with the slowest rate of vibration and the longest wavelength. Known to be able to raise blood pressure, red can strengthen and stimulate the body. Red is associated with the planet Mars and the element of Fire, and also with love, desire, motivation, power, arousal, inspiration, activity, war and success. It is a warm to hot colour which is symbolic of life, strength and vitality. Red is a powerful energiser and stimulant and has the ability to contract energy. It is the colour of passion, intensity and sexuality, conjuring up feelings of excitement and danger.

Psychologically red can help make us feel warm and activated. Red is connected with the Root or Base Chakra, located at the base of the spine, which is associated with security and survival and grounds you to the physical reality of your life. It will revitalise your whole energy system, alleviate exhaustion, boost energy and promote boldness; red is the great revitaliser, restorer and replenisher. Red is also associated with emotional outbursts, eroticism, anger and stimulation. Frustration and resentment can ferment and then explode as anger or violence if too much red is in your environment.

On a more subdued level, these can fester into restlessness, impatience and irritation. Red has good and bad connotations; 'red letter days', Dorothy's ruby slippers, 'rolling out the red carpet', Little Red Riding Hood's cape, and 'painting the town red' imply richness, adventure and vitality, but holding a 'red rag to a bull', red herrings, 'seeing red' and being 'in the red' aren't such positive connections. Additionally, red is recognised as the colour of both Cupid and the Devil. It can also burn out or scorch you with its heat. However, red is often given bad press and dismissed as being 'unspiritual' because it is connected to our primitive instincts and desires and governs our fight-or-flight adrenal glands, linking one to all things material and to the Earth itself. But these are all an integral part of your journey, and when the path gets too wearing and dispiriting, red can re-endow you with motivation, confidence, energy and joie de vivre!

★ ORANGE ★

"Orange is the happiest colour in the world."
Frank Sinatra

Planetary Association ★ The Sun

Complementary Colour ★ Blue

Healing Qualities ★ Antidepressant, Stimulating, Creativity, Confidence, Positivity, Laughter, Transformation, Sociability, Constructiveness

Keywords ★ Healing, Uplifting, Playfulness, Fun, Flirtatious (red + yellow), Positive Thinking, Justice, Legal Matters, Emotional Strength, Prosperity, Self Esteem, Zest, Determination, Sociability, Energy, Enthusiasm

Strong, rich, stimulating, warming and packed with positive vibrations, orange inspires achievement, joy, delight and gentle confidence. Orange has an energising vibe, promoting confidence and wellbeing. An effective antidepressant, it encourages creativity and passion, and alleviates feelings of nervousness. Orange is the symbol of feminine energy, the energy of creation. It is gentler than the dynamic energy of red, but energy-wise, they are complementary.

Combining the passion of red with the wisdom of yellow, orange is the colour of joy, zest and of dance, giving freedom to thoughts and feelings, and disperses heaviness, allowing the body natural, joyful movements. Having the ability to bring about changes in biochemical structure, orange has the capacity to disperse depression. It can be used to attract attention, signal danger and even magnetise prosperity *. Some special animals that are this colour are tigers, monarch butterflies, orang-utans (the 'people of the forest'), ginger cats and goldfish.

Orange is also a feature and predominant colour in some of nature's most spectacular sights and phenomena: sunsets, Autumn leaves, the Northern Lights, the Grand Canyon, Uluru, the ancient city of Petra and the Egyptian Pyramids to name a few. Orange is the colour of the saffron robes of Buddhism and carries with it deep insight and a profound understanding of the bliss of pure 'being', of simply living, laughing and enjoying the present moment. If you lack this simple happy vibe, orange bears the dual significance of mellow profundity and an insatiable appetite for life and living, and imparts both expansiveness and relaxation, helping you to feel more vibrant and easy going. Orange's vibratory rate is connected with the Sacral Chakra, located below the navel, and is connected with physical, sexual and material desires. Orange, as well as gold, is associated with Leo, and also the other two Fire signs, symbolising the fiery nature of these signs through such concepts as glowing embers or licking flames. It is also connected to the planet Mercury. Working with orange-coloured crystals can help bring more inspiration, self-esteem and emotional strength into your experience. Although it is generally a positive colour, avoid it if you are feeling crowded, sick, frustrated or claustrophobic. Overall, orange demands attention, exuding confidence, enthusiasm and warmth.

* Orange trees and their blossoms are symbols of generosity and purity. In some traditions, this tree even signifies the Tree of Knowledge of good and evil Paradise. In some magical belief systems, it is thought that placing a bowl of oranges upon a central dining table attracts wealth and prosperity into the home.

Red and orange, and their respective complementary rainbow spectrum complementary colours, turquoise and blue, are Aries's special LUCKY colours! These shades can be worn or otherwise used together to dazzling and mesmerising effect.

ARIES' CHAKRA CORRESPONDENCE ★ SOLAR PLEXUS

The word 'chakra' comes from the Sanskrit and means 'wheel', disc' or 'circle'. Chakras are vitally important to your physical health, emotional wellbeing and spiritual growth, and are regarded as a complete integrated system that works holistically. The chakras are funnel-shaped spinning energy vortexes of multi-coloured light. These swirling vortexes of energy absorb and distribute life-force, the subtle energy known as *prana*. The seven master chakras - Root, Sacral, Solar Plexus, Heart, Throat, Third Eye and Crown - lie in the centre line of the body, with the first five embedded within the spinal column. Each chakra vibrates at a different vibrational frequency and on a different note, and responds to specific life issues or 'thought forms'.

The lower body chakras deal with physical issues. As we move up the body, the chakras correspond to increasingly spiritual concerns. As a consequence, each chakra's energy vibrates at a different rate, depending on whether they govern earthbound or ethereal issues. The lower chakras have slower and denser vibrations, while the higher chakras spin at faster speeds with higher vibrations.

Because the chakras have no physical manifestation and cannot be located using any scientific instrument, they have tended to be viewed with scepticism by many Western medical professionals, a distinction they share with energy points in acupuncture and the notion of meridians. Instead, they are believed to have been sensed intuitively by many people over many centuries, and indeed people in yoga positions and in deep meditation have reported experiencing the sensation of a surge of energy rising from the base of the spine and emerging through the top of the head. Some people have even said they have seen points of blue light when their *kundalini* energy has risen from the lowest chakra to the highest, as well as experiencing a profound sense of happiness and ecstasy.

In summary, the Universal Life Force enters the body through the Crown chakra at the top of the head. As it works its way through the body, it flows through the other centres. As it spreads to the Base chakra, it is said to arouse the kundalini energy, which yogis believe sleeps in a coiled serpentine form.

The chakra associated with Aries is the third, or Solar Plexus chakra, which governs confidence, personal power and control.

SOLAR PLEXUS CHAKRA

Location ★ Behind the Navel
Colour ★ Yellow
Concerned with ★ Personal Power, Confidence & Control
Gland ★ Adrenals
Essential Oils ★ Chamomile, Neroli, Bergamot, Benzoin, Clary Sage, Dill, Palmarosa, Cypress, Fennel, Lemon, Hyssop, Juniper, Marjoram, Sage, Black Pepper
Animal ★ Ram
Shape ★ Downward Triangle
Element ★ Fire

Planets ★ Mars, Sun
Zodiac Signs ★ Aries, Leo
Flower ★ 10-petalled Lotus
Energy State ★ Plasma
Mantra ★ RAM

Positive Expression ★ Intelligent, optimistic, forgiving, thoughtful, perceptive

Negative Expression (Blockage) ★ Impractical, daydreaming, imbalance between the heart and head, lack of confidence, difficulty manifesting desires, low self-esteem, misuse of power, over-reliance on will, dominance, shame

The Solar Plexus chakra is located at the diaphragm. Its Sanskrit name is *manipura*, and its symbol is a ten-petal yellow lotus flower whose centre contains a red downward-pointing triangle. Balance in this chakra is expressed as self-confidence, a feeling of personal empowerment, logical thought processes and goal manifestation. It corresponds to the pancreas and the Solar nerve plexus. Crystals that can be used to cleanse and balance this chakra are mostly yellow stones, including: Citrine, Amber, Ametrine, Yellow Jasper, Amblygonite, Golden Beryl, Sunstone, Yellow Sapphire, Tiger's Eye and Yellow Tourmaline.

LUCKY CAREER TIPS & PATHS THAT WILL MAKE YOUR BANK BALANCE & SPIRITUAL SELF SOAR

The branch of astrology known as 'vocational astrology' encompasses the areas of one's calling, career path, or ideal profession. Careers, jobs, professions and occupations can all mean different things to different people, but to simplify the definition, I refer to a vocation as one's true calling, one's authentic path, and a dynamic way of life which pays an income in some form and leads to a deep fulfilment of personal and spiritual needs. An ideal vocation will provide self-fulfilment, ego satisfaction, and feed one's inner drive to achieve what they ultimately wish to achieve, whether that be to gain recognition, wealth or approval, to travel, to learn and fulfil an inner need for knowledge, an urge to serve others in some way, or an urge to improve personal, societal or universal conditions.

In order to gain ultimate fulfilment and self-esteem, we all need a purpose in life. Many people gain this through their work, providing the job or career they choose suits their temperament, talents and aspirations. If our professional life is unsatisfactory or disharmonious in any way, frustration, unhappiness and even despair can result. Although your whole horoscope would need to be drawn up and interpreted in order to gain more substantial, deeper insights into your ideal career and purpose, you can begin by being guided by your Sun sign, which can give you many pointers to a suitable, and therefore successful, career path. You just never know, something in the following might jump out at you and make your soul dance immediately - and hopefully all the way to the bank!

With your Sun in Aries, you like to be the leader in almost anything you do. Your inborn talents for leadership and inspiring others are your greatest strengths, and your talent for leadership in particular actually improves as you learn to cooperate with others. As in any area of life, in work you love a challenge, work well under pressure and never shrink from danger. Needing plenty of activity and stimulation, your ideal vocation gives you the opportunity to be active in mind and body, independence, freedom of thought and movement, a healthy degree of autonomy, champion a cause, and a chance to capitalise on your enterprising and energetic nature.

You like to be active, either mentally or physically, and will quickly become bored with routine or a dreary, slow workplace. Monotony and small details are your biggest enemies, and because you have plenty of initiative and enthusiasm, you should avoid any occupation which is slow-paced, tedious or requires patience, precision or perfection. You have a great need to forge ahead and dislike limits or restrictions on your boundless vitality and mind that is bristling with ideas.

Ariens are particularly suited to owning and operating their own business, for three reasons: you can lead rather than follow, being your own boss means you are in control, and it provides a challenge which will always bring the best out of your fighting spirit. If you work for a large company, working in areas or positions where there are opportunities for promotion and advancement would be ideal, as you are capable of rapidly climbing any ladder. If opportunities do not abound or present themselves, you are just as swift to become bored and move on to something bigger and better.

The Ram is naturally drawn to danger and novelty, and as you are impetuous and enthusiastic about anything new, you are inclined to jump into careers head first without thinking it through first; but if it does turn out to be ill-suited to you, you find out sooner than later.

Because your ruler is Mars, the god of war, and with your love of danger, innovations, discovery and novelty, occupations which involve adventure, crime, emergencies, surgery, pioneering, exploration, action, medical experiments, firearms, mining, competition, destruction and construction, machinery, metals, motivation, leadership, physical effort, sport and stamina, will more than likely hold appeal for you.

Being an energetic sign who can inspire activity in others, Ariens also make good foremen, supervisors and directors, as long as they are given positions of authority. You must command others, otherwise you risk losing interest in what you are doing. And as in every other aspect of your life, you are best at the beginning of a project, but because you cannot maintain your enthusiasm, you often leave the completion or finer details of the job up to others. As you have ample self-confidence and the ability to uplift others, you would ultimately make a great coach who teaches, guides, motivates or trains others. Advertising, public relations, broadcasting and television (especially adventure, lifestyle or reality programs) may also appeal to your spirit of adventure. Your lively mind and direct approach would make a surprisingly efficient psychiatrist.

For Ariens, the following fields or occupations may attract your attention: Engineering, Extreme Adventure Tour Operator, Mechanical Work, Politics, the Armed Forces, Butcher, Metal Worker, Explorer, Firefighting, Police Force/Law Enforcement, Arms Manufacturer, Soldier, Dentist, Professional Athlete/Sportsperson, Rally Driver, Motivational/Inspirational Speaker, and any work requiring enterprise and initiative.

Whichever career path you choose, you tend to be very ambitious, assertive and are likely to attain all your wildest goals - as long as you keep your impatience in check and don't expect the world to fall into your lap overnight (even though it often does)!

LUCKY PLACES WHERE YOUR ENERGY IS HEIGHTENED

As the Fire element and Choleric humour corresponds with hot and dry conditions, warm, arid and low-humidity places suit your constitution, disposition and temperament. The following nations, countries and cities are also places whose vibrations are closely allied with the sign of Aries:

Israel, Iran, Luxembourg, Germany, Palestine, England, France (Burgundy), Poland (Krakow), Italy (Florence, Naples, Padua), Haiti and North America (Las Vegas, Brunswick). South Africa, Lithuania, Mongolia, Sierra Leone, Morocco, Czech Republic, Japan, Syria, Bangladesh, Canada and Zimbabwe, are also in tune with the Arien energy, as are all capital cities and sporting facilities and any places where battles are fought or have been won, or empires have been built. Any extreme adventure holiday, a road trip across Wild West America with an obligatory stop at Las Vegas and the Grand Canyon, a drive along Australia's famous Nullarbor Plain, or a desert trek on camelback (think Central Australia or Saudi Arabia) or somewhere where the climate is hot and dry (while you are there at least!) and that offers plenty of action and novelty, could very well be your ticket to Arien heaven!

GEMS & CRYSTALS

"People love stones, and apparently stones love people. Like the angels they may be, they seem endlessly willing to serve the wellbeing of humans and to help us achieve our desires …Unlike people of the ancient past, we now have access to virtually the entire mineral kingdom. We have the opportunity to work like modern alchemists, combining and arranging the stones and their currents, looking for combinations and patterns that can help us enhance our inner and outer lives."
Robert Simmons, *Stones of the New Consciousness*

Each crystal and mineral of the Earth embodies different qualities, patterns or potential expressions of the Divine language, the silent whispers of the Universe. If we can accept the fact that the human body is a sophisticated, multi-faceted antenna system comprised of a crystalline matrix that is constantly transmitting and receiving all manner of energies, it could then be assumed that energy and body workers who use quartz, shells and stones, which are also crystalline materials, have the power to promote resonant interactions with the liquid 'crystal' structures found in human tissues. It could even be said that we are all made of essentially the same substances and structures, and that crystals and gemstones vibrate at varying energetic levels which can connect with our own in order to 'buzz' and dance together to make a harmonious Universe both within and without.

All crystals work through vibrational balancing and by channelling energy. The magic of crystals is in their colour, which is determined by the rate at which their atoms vibrate; these vibrations can be matched to the energy given by your own body's aura. And just as light can be focused and refracted through gemstones, so too can all kinds of psychic energy, from healing energies to Divine communications.

Gemstones can help us attune to higher vibrations and bring them into our own experience and being. This theory of crystal resonance suggests that the characteristic energy patterns emanated by any stone can be transferred into the 'liquid crystal medium' of our bodies through resonance. Our bodies, being composed of these tuneable liquids, can mimic and mirror any consistent vibrational pattern with which we come into contact; we can therefore resonate with the healthful qualities of various crystals and minerals.

Crystals and precious stones have been valued throughout world cultures over many centuries for their healing virtues and capacities to imbue courage, strength, invulnerability, clairvoyance, love and numerous other qualities. Wearing gemstones is one of the simplest and most effective self-healing practices you can undertake, and wearing or carrying those stones whose vibrations correspond with the qualities you wish to embody brings their energetic currents into engagement with your body.

Over time the phenomenon of energetic integration, may be felt tangibly and your own vibrational field may internalise the stone's currents and adjust to them and effectively 'store' them, making them, eventually, a part of your own vibrational make-up. And we seem to know from the resonances we feel within our bodies when in contact with these gemstones, that crystals emanate tangible, if oft immeasurable, currents.

Crystals act as transmitters and amplifiers of your will or intentions - as long as your will or intentions are in sympathy with the crystal's energy. The mineral kingdom refers to stones, minerals and crystals and the associations and vibrations they carry. When working with stones, we are working with several different layers of spiritual energies, and although they can be regarded as inanimate 'psychic batteries', they are actually moving, vibrating masses of energy which transmit potential and power into our lives. Some crystals and stones even have receptive powers, which means they can absorb energy and retain it within until cleansed or re-programmed.

Although it is untrue that the only stones you can usefully wear are the ones astrologically matched with your Sun sign or ruling planet, those which align with your Sun sign or ruling planet are your most fortuitous and therefore strongest 'attractors' and 'amplifiers'.

Twelve oracular gemstones were described in the Bible, as the author of *Exodus* (28-15 and 17-21) knew them. Yahweh spoke to Moses about the breastplate he would have to wear to train for priesthood, and described it to him in these words: "And thou shalt make the breastplate of judgement with cunning work; ... And thou shalt set in it settings of stones, even four rows of stones; the first row shall be a sardius, a topaz, and a carbuncle. And the second row shall be an emerald, a sapphire and a diamond. And the third row an opal, an agate and an amethyst. And the fourth row a beryl, and an onyx, and a jasper; they shall be set in hold in their inclosings. And the stones shall be with the children … (all) twelve (of them)." Given that the compilers of the Bible lived during a time when astrological belief was prevalent in Babylon, it seems valid to assert that these previously named gemstones would have some astrological basis. Further, since these ancient people supposedly made correlations between each of the twelve precious stones, and one of the twelve zodiac signs, there are seven crystalline systems set down in crystallography (or the science of the laws which influence the formation, structure and geometric, physical and chemical properties of crystallised matter) as analogous with the seven traditional ruling planets of the zodiac.

However, nobody is under the rule of one planet alone. We are all in essence a complex mixture of every planet, many elements and varying aspects, depending on their positions, placements and prominence in our birth chart. Everything that goes on in the skies above us affects what is going on here on Earth, and also *within* us. Your lucky stones are to assist you to tune into your Sun sign's energy and planetary influences, but you are by no means limited to the ones listed for your sign alone. Above all, let your stones, whichever ones you choose, work for you and allow them to transport your very own unique and magical energy into the wider Universe.

> "Beautiful and strong is the material of stones, but more beautiful and much more powerful is the mystery that emanates from them."
> **Chinese Poet & Alchemist, Li Po, 8th Century A.D.**

★ CLEAR QUARTZ ★

The Master Healer ★ *For All Zodiac Signs*

A common, well-known and popular gem, clear quartz (sometimes known as rock crystal) is an all-purpose 'jack-of-all-trades' stone. It amplifies the magic of any work you do or wishes you make. It is connected with all the chakras and increases the power of all other crystals. Clear quartz is a deep soul cleanser, which unblocks and regulates energy and emotions on all levels. It is balancing and harmonising. In various cultures, quartz crystal is reputed to be the most powerful crystal, the 'grandfather crystal', and the 'chief of the Stone People'. Clear quartz is also considered to be the only gemstone that is modifiable to suit your needs *, as other crystals automatically contain and retain their own specific resonance or natural signature. In essence, clear quartz is the most easily programmable and the most overall healing and readily accessible crystals of the mineral kingdom, holding a unique importance in the Universe of gems. And because of its all-encompassing nature and wide-ranging healing abilities, it has zodiacal affinities with all the signs.

* To program your clear quartz crystal, simply hold it on your Third Eye chakra (between and just above the

physical eyes) and concentrate on the purpose for which you wish to use it. Be positive and receptive while you allow your crystal to fill with this energy. If you wish, you could also state the intention of the programming out loud, for example, 'I program this crystal for love / healing / meditation / abundance / protection or (insert your own word here)'. You could also run your clear quartz crystal under running water, allow it to dry naturally, then hold the stone with both hands, bring it up to your mouth and blow into it sharply three times in order to impregnate it with your own breath. Then, hold it firmly in one hand and silently invite and welcome it into your life as a friend, helper and guide.

ARIEN & MARTIAN LUCKY CRYSTALS, STONES & GEMS

Aries birth stones ★ Ruby, Bloodstone, Aquamarine, Diamond

March birth stones ★ Jasper, Bloodstone, Aquamarine

April birth stones ★ Sapphire, Diamond, Zircon

Ruby, Bloodstone, Aquamarine and Diamond (your four primary birthstones), Red Coral (for Mars), Jasper, Sapphire and Zircon (March and April birthstones) are your luckiest stones, and one of these gems should be worn about your person to ensure good luck and increase your magnetism. Hematite, Iron Pyrite, Magnetite, Aventurine, Carnelian, Fire Agate, Citrine, Amethyst, Kunzite, Apache Tear, Kyanite, Flint, Tibetan Quartz, Malachite,

Rhodochrosite, Mahogany Obsidian, Lapis Lazuli, Titanium Quartz, Emerald, Tektite, Orange Spinel, Topaz, Garnet, Red Jasper and Pink Tourmaline also align with Aries' energy.

CRYSTALS & THE PLANETS

All the Vedic texts agree in relating gems to planets. This verse from the *Jatax Parijat* links each gem to a planet:

'The ruby is the gem of the Lord of the Day (the Sun),
The shining pearl is the gem of the cold Moon,
Red coral is the gem of Mars,
The emerald is the gem of noble Mercury,
Yellow sapphire is the gem of Jupiter, instructor of gods,
Diamond is the gem of Venus, instructor of demons,
Blue sapphire is the gem of Saturn.'

Each planet influences its gem, and their curative power varies according to the position of its planet in the zodiac. Ayurvedic medicine has always paid attention to these details in their healing practices, often advising people to wear their corresponding zodiacal stone as a ring or a talisman.

CRYSTALS & THE ELEMENTS

Crystals are inextricably linked to the four elements, from their original creation to their potency and use in magical rituals and healing. Formed by the combination, in varying conditions, of different physical elements, such as metals, non-metals and gases, some stones require the enormous heat generated by volcanoes or deep thermal currents to bond their molecular makeup, while others may require pressure or water sources. The effects of the four elements of Fire, Earth, Air and Water is evident in these formation processes. The heat generated by Fire, pressure from the Earth, and the chemical reactions involved in absorbing elements from the Air and Water, all demonstrate the four elements in action to produce the correct conditions and ingredients necessary for the creation of crystals, lending them each their unique qualities.

CRYSTALS & THE FIRE ELEMENT

The transformational influence of Fire can be seen in such examples as citrine, which is formed when heat is applied to amethyst, and obsidian, which is created through astonishing volcanic temperatures. Although Fire can be a destructive force, its effect is also to change things, and it is this transformative energy which can be harnessed in Fire-inspired gemstones to help facilitate positive changes in your life, through meditation, chakra balancing or other magical rituals.

Some Fiery crystals are ★ Calcite, Ruby, Amber, Obsidian, Garnet, Citrine, Bloodstone (Heliotrope), Topaz, Spinel and Pyrite.

THE CRYSTALLINE SYSTEM OF YOUR RULING PLANET MARS

Associated with your ruling planet Mars, are Amethyst, Magnetite, Cornelian, Barite, Garnet, Ruby, Topaz and Bloodstone. This is the third crystalline system, known as orthorhombic, that is having a rectangular parallelepiped. The stone which perhaps represents this system best is Topaz, which was famous for the good fortune it brought to those who wore it, but also for its therapeutic properties in treating and even healing eye-related conditions.

MARS' GEMSTONE ASSOCIATION

★ **Red Coral** ★ Coral is among the most ancient of gem materials and was first used for adornment in prehistoric times. The name comes from a Greek word that means 'nymph of the sea'. Long regarded as a powerful talisman that was able to stop bleeding, give protection from evil spirits and even ward off hurricanes, red coral is renowned for its strength and energy. The wearing of coral was reputed to cure or prevent many ailments, and as an amulet it banished nightmares, protected children and warded off demons of the darkness, so in this sense it could be used as a protective gem. The coral used in jewellery is the hard skeleton formed by certain polyps of the corallium nobile family and occurs in red, blue, golden, black, white and pink. These polyps are minute living creatures that live in vast colonies. When they die, their skeletal remains - mostly calcium carbonate - build up to form massive coral reefs. Red coral is considered the best colour for protective charms and is called 'Witch Stone' in Italy. It was thought to absorb emotional negativity and was used against the Evil Eye. Coral, particularly red coral, encourages one to have more determination and courage. As an ocean dweller, coral's astrological correspondence is with the Moon, which also befits its watery genesis. When sourcing your coral, however, you should bear in mind that coral reefs are among the world's most vital yet fragile ecosystems and materials taken from them should only be purchased from a sustainable marine operator.

ARIES' FEATURE CRYSTAL ★ DIAMOND

'King of the Crystals'

Diamond is pure crystallised carbon and is known as the ruler of the mineral kingdom, due to its hardwearing qualities, hardness and sheer brilliance. Diamond is the purest substance in nature and one of the hardest (10 out of 10 on the Mohs scale). The word 'diamond' has its origin in the Greek word 'adamas', which means unconquerable. Mined for over 4,000 years, ancient civilisations discovered that this amazing gem could cut any other stone. The diamond is known universally as a token of love; quite simply, it is the ultimate symbol of purity. This luminously brilliant gem, through its renowned purity and durability, offers incomparable proof of total perfection expressed in a single element. Its pure white light can help to bring your life into a cohesive whole, the first step in using your power to optimum effect. It bonds relationships, is said to enhance the love of a husband to his wife, brings love and clarity into a partnership, and is seen as a sign of commitment and faithfulness.

Psychologically, this precious gem imparts a sense of fearlessness, fortitude and invincibility, for diamonds are unbreakable in every sense of the word. Diamond is also an amplifier of any energy with which it comes into contact, therefore should only be used for positive spells and magic, and is one of the few stones that never needs recharging or cleansing; in fact, it increases the energy of whatever it comes into contact with and is very effective when used with other crystals for healing as it enhances and draws out their power. Like the clear quartz, it is a master healer which accelerates the spiritual development of its wearer. As an amplifier of energy, the merciless light of diamond will highlight anything that is negative and requires transformation. Diamond has been a symbol for wealth for thousands of years and is one of the stones of manifestation, with the ability to attract abundance; the larger the diamond, the more abundance will be drawn to the requester.

Diamond helps to clear emotional and mental pain, alleviates fear and brings about new beginnings. It also provides a link between the intellect and the higher mind, aiding clarity and enlightenment of mind. On a spiritual level, it allows one's soul light to shine out, cleansing the aura of anything shrouding the inner light, and reminds you of your soul's aspirations; it activates the Crown chakra, linking it to the 'Divine light'. Indeed, clear crystals such as diamond will interact with your energy field by raising your vibration through clearing away any cloudiness or blockages within your subtle bodies. With it may be worn a bloodstone, another Arien gemstone, when the beneficent influence of the diamond will be greatly increased. A highly creative stone, stimulating imagination and inventiveness, and aiding spiritual evolution, it seems it was made for the pioneering, strong-as-steel, dynamic Arien nature.

ARIEN POWER CRYSTALS

Around six thousand years ago, in ancient Mesopotamia, the Sumerians started studying precious stones and minerals, as well as the stars, with a view of improving their lives in many ways by probing the secrets and mysteries of the Universe. Their esoteric interests and knowledge were such that they began to grasp the general connections between the Earth and the heavens, or the Solar system as they knew it, and the functions of stones and minerals as a link between the two. Their method of making these connections was by colour (for example the Sun was allocated all yellow stones), as well as other spiritual links. The gemstones listed for the portion of your zodiac sign are given their status as your 'power crystals' due to the links that can be made between your primary planetary ruler/s and your mutable planetary ruler (listed last), and each stone's particular colour, chemical and mineral compositions, healing properties, and the number they are given (based on the Mohs scale of hardness: for example, diamond scores a perfect 10 out of 10), all of which combine to align with your planetary rulers. Working mindfully with your planet's special crystals is one way you can increase the flow of power and magic into your life.

POWER CRYSTALS FOR FIRST HALF
ARIENS ★ (20 March - 3 April)

Influenced by Mars and the Sun

Pink Diamond, Pink Sapphire, Sunstone, Bloodstone (Heliotrope), Plasma, Jasper, Cinnabar, Dolomite, Pearl Spar Quartz

★ **SUNSTONE** ★ The two main types of sunstone are orange sunstone and yellow sunstone, sometimes known as golden labradorite. In some, a reddish iridescence, brought about by a minute inclusion of hematite and other minerals on a yellow or brownish-yellow background, is characteristic of this cheerful gem. The sunstone imitates the Sun by its red and gold spangled brilliance which glitters and gleams. This stone represented the Sun god in ancient Greece and in some Native American rituals of the medicine wheel, it is placed in the centre and said to glow. This is an alchemical stone traditionally linked to the benevolent gods, good luck and fortune. It also helps facilitate a profound connection to light and the regenerative powers of the Sun itself.

Yellow sunstone has an affinity for the Solar Plexus chakra and removes stress, anxiety and fear from this energy centre, suffusing it with light. An uplifting crystal, sunstone can fill you with love, laughter, confidence and inspiration. Its magical properties include magnetising abundance and all that you wish for, instilling an optimistic outlook, and even helping with bereavement and wistful reminiscing about the 'good old days' that can make one unable to enjoy the present. It is a joyful, light-inspiring stone that brings about joie de vivre and good nature and enhances intuitive function. If life has lost its lustre, sunstone can help restore the shine, by clearing all the chakras and allowing the true self to shine through. As a stone of good cheer, it can help dispel negative influences around you which are embedded in your aura or your chakras, removing the draining effects of other people, lovingly returning the contact to the other person through tie-cutting. It assists with removing co-dependency tendencies, procrastination and depression, and facilitates independence, vitality and self-empowerment.

Emotionally, sunstone can lift dark moods and is effective for seasonal affective disorder (SAD), and encourages enthusiasm and lightens the darkness of winter. When placed upon the Solar Plexus chakra which it aligns most strongly with, sunstone can extract heavy or repressed emotions and transmute them. It is helpful to help you move forward when you feel blocked on life's path, encouraging exploration of your possibilities and aiding spiritual expansion. It can remove the feeling of being limited in personal power or potential, opening you up to new options. Overall, it stimulates self-healing powers, inspires optimism and harmonises all the organs. Interestingly, and as its name suggests, sunstone is particularly useful when used in the Sun.

★ **BLOODSTONE** ★ Also known as heliotrope, from the Greek words 'helios' meaning 'Sun', and 'trepein', meaning 'to turn towards', this alternate name stems from the belief in Ancient Greece and China that heliotrope could detect Solar eclipses, indicating the presence of the Moon as it approached the Sun. Holding mightier than Mars energy but still relating to that planet, the bloodstone, with its traces of Plutonian influence, can give off an intense energy, and weigh heavily on the mind - for that reason, in healing it should always be used in combination with the more calming energies of clear or rose quartz, which will alleviate its oppressive effects.

According to myths, bloodstone has the power to detect changes in the heavens and therefore, is able to shroud things from view. The use of bloodstone stems from Ancient Babylon and Egypt, but the tale of its legendary origins are arguably more astounding than its powers. The blood of Christ, as he hung on the cross, was said to have splashed onto a piece of jasper below, tinging it with red and turning it into bloodstone. From this auspicious origin, this gemstone has been credited with the power to heal all manner of ailments, such as tumours, poor circulation, haemorrhaging, bloodshot eyes, snake bites, haemorrhoids, and even to protect the wearer from poison. The Egyptians believed that bloodstone could protect against deception, and worn as a protective amulet, it could help you see through lies.

This is a dark green gemstone variety of chalcedony, a green jasper with red flecks, is symbolic of courage, and it is thought to bring its wearers good fortune. Bloodstone has a variety of other magical abilities, including the power to stop blood from coming out of the body, increasing blood flow within the body, enabling one to see the truth, win legal battles and reminds us of our eternal connection to all living things. This stone can inspire bravery and, being aligned with Solar and Martian forces and sacred powers of healing, bloodstone is a useful crystal to work with to energise, protect, empower and calm. It is also said to inspire bravery, fuel your ambition and help you overcome inertia to improve your work life in particular. It is believed to break down deep-rooted diseases and counteract overindulgence, obsession, violence and aggression, but in its lighter aspects, the bloodstone encourages a sunny disposition as it sweeps 'debris' from the chakras.

Other magical properties ascribed to this stone include realigning one with one's spiritual purpose, calming scattered thoughts, assisting in regeneration of the physical body, enhancing creativity, helping to make decisions, and as well as imparting strength during periods of difficult or loss of hope. As it is connected with the Base or Root Chakra, as well as the Heart chakra (it is an excellent aid to grounding heart energy), it can give your lust and sex drive a boost, and increase your libido, clearing any blockages which may be restricting sexual expression or desire. Overall, it has beneficial effects on the heart, blood and circulatory system. Used as a healing stone for over 5,000 years, it maintains the energetic purity of the blood, which in ancient times was regarded as the Life Force. As its name suggests, bloodstone is an excellent blood cleanser, detoxifier and an overall powerful healer.

★ **JASPER** ★ Jasper is a chalcedony which comes in a variety of colours - brown, orange, red, yellow and green being the most common. The green colour when flecked with red, is known as bloodstone. Each colour corresponds with a different chakra, and all can be used for aligning the chakras, promoting wellbeing and overall healing. The Ancients believed in its power to lighten the spirit, bring comfort, to relax and even make childbirth easier. Jasper has been used in charms around the world for many centuries; from Ancient Greece and Egypt to the Americas, jasper was considered a sacred and protective stone which was worn or carried to protect the bearer from misfortune, such as from a range of maladies including poisoning, insanity, 'possession' and evil spirits. Green jasper has traditionally been associated with luck - a jasper arrowhead was said to bring the bearer good fortune, and a green jasper talisman with the symbol of Aquarius engraved on it was carried by traders to enhance their sales.

Red jasper has balancing and grounding properties and is attuned to the Base Chakra, bestowing courage and the willpower to achieve one's goals. Excellent for stimulating the circulation and increasing energy, red jasper is also a nurturing stone that is helpful in times of recovery. It also cleanses and stabilises the aura and strengthens your boundaries. Yellow jasper balances the Solar Plexus chakra, calms the nerves and is an overall protective stone, protecting during both spiritual and physical travel 'journeys'. Both grounding and stabilising, this stone has a special ability to take control of uncontrolled or unfocused energy. Having a grounding energy makes this stone useful for connecting with the Earth and focusing one's thoughts on solidity and form. Also protective, wearing or carrying jasper can make you less susceptible to negative influences, such as being the subject of slander or gossip.

Jasper has had a long reputation as a healing stone and also as a rain-bringer. Emotionally, it absorbs negativity and aligns the chakras and the aura. It imparts determination and encourages assertiveness and honesty with oneself. It also stimulates the imagination and transforms ideas into action. It can help fight anxiety and inspire confidence. Overall, jasper is known as the 'supreme nurturer', supporting and sustaining during times of stress, and bringing tranquillity and wholeness to one's spirit.

★ **CINNABAR** ★ Alchemy, magic, transformation, wealth, insight, manifestation, mental agility are all key words for this mixture of red cinnabar, white quartz and other trace minerals. Its element is Fire and it is connected with the Base, Sacral and Third Eye chakras. A very attractive stone, its colour is usually vermilion or scarlet red. It forms around volcanic vents and hot springs and may also occur in sedimentary rocks associated with recent volcanic activity. The gentle Martian world with its light atmosphere, is in harmony with this rock's vermilion crystals, and cinnabar is often found in veins cooling near volcanic disturbances, corresponding with the extinct volcanoes on Mars. Cinnabar becomes cinnabar quartz when it forms in conjunction with quartz, and cinnabar quartz is the most beneficial form of cinnabar for metaphysical use. The quartz serves to increase the durability of the stone, as well as magnifying cinnabar's energetic properties.

Cinnabar on its own attracts abundance and increases persuasiveness, as well as assisting organisation, business and finance. It imparts fluency of the mind and speech, releases energy blockages and aligns energy centres. As a stone of the Magician archetype, cinnabar (or cinnabar quartz) can facilitate the alignment of personal will with Divine will, allowing one to 'tweak' the Divine currents so that one can influence the form of creative material manifestation. Cinnabar is also aligned with the god Mercury, also known as Hermes or Thoth, and as such it can help increase mental agility, intellectual brilliance and clarity of thought, traits for which these gods were known.

The usual colour of cinnabar, pure red, is resonant with the colour of one of the images of the Philosopher's Stone, the 'attainment' of which is the goal of alchemy. This is the Stone of the 'lovers of wisdom' (*philo* = love; *sopher* = wisdom, or Sophia), which helps the alchemists attain one of their loftiest aims aside from transmuting lead to gold - that of wisdom. For one's aspirations of spiritual growth and evolution, cinnabar is a potent quickener, helping to speed up the process by which one's transformation occurs. Overall, it facilitates the process of alchemical change within the individual and brings about the experience and expression of one's newfound inner golden illuminated awareness. Cinnabar, along with other abundance-attracting crystals such as topaz, sunstone, carnelian, jade and turquoise, has thousands of years of historical use as charms and amulets to support its manifesting powers.

* Cinnabar and cinnabar quartz contain Mercury, so caution should be exercised when handling this crystal.

POWER CRYSTALS FOR SECOND HALF
ARIENS ★ (4 - 19 April)

Influenced by Mars and Jupiter
Alexandrite, Rhodonite, Bowenite, Carnelian (Sard), Youngite, Ruby Zoisite

★ **ALEXANDRITE** ★ Alexandrite is a variety of chrysoberyl, a beryllium aluminium oxide with a hardness of 8.5. One of the hardest gemstones, second only to diamond and corundum, its crystal pattern is orthorhombic. Alexandrite is a crystal of contrasts. It opens the intuition and metaphysical abilities, and creates a strong will and personal magnetism. One of the world's rarest gemstones, the finest specimens of alexandrite are costlier than diamonds - and its price understandably reflects its rarity. Discovered in the Ural Mountains of Russia in around 1830 on the birthday of Czar Alexander II and named after him, its key words are joy, wisdom and release of sorrow.

A notable feature of this crystal is its stunning optical property of colour change - it is light red or red-purple in incandescent artificial light, and green (often an intense grass-green) or blue-green in daylight. Since green is the colour of new growth and pink the shade of impartial love, the Russian name for Alexandrite, 'Stone of Good Omen', could not be more apt. This stone has a positive electrical charge which stays for hours after rubbing, and an energy factor which changes with its colour. But potent though this stone looks, it radiates sensitivity. In physical healing, it bypasses the actual condition and goes directly to the root of it and balances any disharmonies out. It is a regenerative stone, aiding the tissues of the body to renew after dis-ease - both internally and externally. It has even been used to treat leukaemia and cancer. These regenerative properties also extend to spiritual transformation and growth, enhancing your ability to find joy in life and aiding psychic protection when undertaking such work. It also carries the beneficial qualities of making one's head feel 'roomier', improving the memory, clearing the eyesight, and relieving any physical tensions. In its colour change, it signifies a spiritual metamorphosis and embodies an inner pattern of flexibility, adaptability and willingness to shift its expression in the presence of varying conditions; it can teach us this very quality in ourselves.

Since its discovery, alexandrite was believed to be a stone of good fortune in its native country. It carries a very joyful vibration and is a powerful agent of inner transformation and spiritual evolution. Primarily stimulating the Crown chakra, it embodies both the heart energy (green) and the higher mind energy (purple). It can stimulate a harmonic opening of the Heart, Third Eye and Crown chakras, during which the three can operate as an integrated whole. Alexandrite's emotional tone is one of exuberant joy. It calls forth the heart's natural state of delighted engagement and teaches us that the spiritual qualities of the celestial realms are also simultaneously here at every moment, encouraging us to take on all the energies that come to us and to do this with a pure commitment to joy. Overall, it centres, reinforces and realigns the mental, emotional and spiritual bodies, enhancing manifestation in all its forms. This precious, rare gem transmits inner peace by developing magnanimity of heart and should be valued and used extensively.

★ **RHODONITE** ★ Rhodonite is a more recently discovered crystal, first found in 1819 and so has no special folklore associated with it. It is a striking pink-violet stone with black colouring that takes its name from the Greek word 'rhodos' meaning 'rose' or 'rose-coloured'. Often found near silver mines, rhodonite can vary from delicate pink to light, rosy red, with its trademark black or gold veins running throughout its structure. As a pink stone, it naturally works well on the Heart chakra and has a positive effect on general health and wellbeing. Because rhodonite is associated with love and friendship, it can be used to attract love into your life by first working on your own self-acceptance and self-love.

Rhodonite works on the principle that when you accept yourself, your energy will attract the love you desire. An emotional balancer that nurtures love and encourages the brotherhood of humanity, it stimulates, clears and activates the Heart chakra. It encourages us to forgive and forget past traumas, allowing the heart to heal, and enables us to express the purity of unconditional love towards both ourselves and others. It also grounds energy and helps one to achieve their potential. Psychologically it helps to heal emotions, and to dispel anxiety, fear and panic attacks. It should be used as soon as possible after a traumatic event to restore balance, calmness and harmony to the wearer. In fact, it can be used as a gem essence to help alleviate shock or trauma (but should never replace experienced medical assistance). It has beneficial effects on the nervous system, so where feelings such as jealousy, anger, bitterness, irritability, selfishness and depression have been suppressed, rhodonite allows them to rise to the surface to be released. It also helps build confidence and self-esteem.

★ **CARNELIAN** ★ Also known as cornelian or sard, carnelian is a type of chalcedony, taking its name from the Latin word 'cornu', which means 'horn', and among the many legendary powers surrounding it, are its remarkable properties as a stone of protection and great spirituality. It varies in colour from pink, orange, and blood-red to brownish or yellow, the colour deepening in direct sunlight. Linked to the Base or Root Chakra, this is a stabilising high-energy stone, and is particularly associated with sexual energy and fertility, said to encourage the kundalini (sexual energy/life force) to be more active; in this way, it could be considered an aphrodisiac. As an activating stone that can help you in realising ideas and making plans manifest, it is a good stone to use if you are trying to become pregnant (both partners should use this crystal while trying to conceive). Carnelian has a strong influence over the female reproductive system. It releases stress and damage that is adversely affecting the etheric body, helps ease the trauma of abuse, and restores and improves the energy flow within the physical body.

Throughout history, carnelian has been used to discern the denizens of the astral plane, and to summon help from its domain. In Buddhism, it represented qualities such as faith, wisdom and perseverance, and in modern times the German literary figure Goethe connected powers of luck, protection, comfort and hope with this stone. The Egyptian *Book of the Dead* is a collection of papyrus scrolls that record in hieroglyphic text the wisdom of ancient priests and the experiences of the soul in the afterlife. Carnelian is mentioned a number of times in this book as it was regarded by the Egyptians as a protective stone and was used in many amulets, particularly those placed on the mummies of the rich and powerful. The carnelian endows its wearer with contentment and self-confidence, and banishes fear, sorrow and the effects of the evil eye. Because it instils a sense of confidence, it can give you the courage to speak your mind, and to overcome shyness, timidity or social inhibitions; it can also help you to trust yourself and your perceptions. It is also excellent for restoring vitality and motivation, and stimulating creativity and dramatic pursuits.

Carnelian can cleanse and re-energise other stones, and along with cinnabar, jade, turquoise, citrine, topaz and sunstone, can create and attract abundance into your experience. Overall, carnelian's signature is strong, stimulating and protective, it is used to repair the etheric body after shock, loss, trauma or betrayal and ameliorates grief, including that associated with bereavement. So if you suffer from existential fears, past physical abuse, rage, resentment, vitality-sapping illness or any long-standing mental anguish, the negativity-banishing properties of this stone are an effective ongoing life-force supplement. Perhaps its lesser known magical quality is that in meditation it can induce a better understanding of the true meaning of life and thus provide a key to wisdom.

★ **RUBY ZOISITE** ★ Zoisite comes in many different colours, including white, brown, yellow, blue, red, green, pink, lavender blue and colourless. In shops, it is often sold with ruby in it, as a variety called ruby zoisite, the presence of ruby increasing its potency. Ruby in zoisite, also called anyolite, is a marriage of passion and patience, between the properties of fiery ruby and earthy zoisite, containing small crystals of ruby which have become embedded within the zoisite stone. Ruby in zoisite is said to enhance fertility, increase vigour, and help overcome laziness. It stimulates psychic abilities when placed on the Crown chakra, amplifying spirituality and engaging the body's own energy field. Ruby in zoisite transmutes negative energy into the positive, being a spiritual comforter particularly helpful for preventing mood swings and periods of grieving. Overall, zoisite is said to encourage creativity and vitality, and put you in touch with what you really enjoy and wish to be doing.

YOUR LUCKY NUMBERS

Your lucky numbers are ★ 7 for Aries ^ & 9 for Mars (also, see 'Lucky Magic Square of Mars')

LUCKY MAGIC SQUARE OF MARS

In Western occult tradition, each planet has traditionally been associated with a series of numbers and particular arrangements of those numbers. One such method of numerological organisation is the magic square. Magic squares date back to ancient times, appearing in China about 3,000 years ago. The first Chinese square is seen in the scroll of the river Lo - the Lo-Shu, a scroll believed to have been created by Fuh-Hi, the mythical founder of Chinese civilisation. Certain squares came to be linked with the planets; these associations came from the Babylonians. Each *kamea*, or magic square, is linked with a particular planet, and each of the squares has a *seal*, which is the geometric pattern created by following the numbers in order of their value. This pattern touches upon all the numbers of the square and the seal is used to represent the entire square. An intelligence and a spirit are also associated with each kamea, derived from the key numbers contained within it, using a Hebrew form of numerology. This intelligence is viewed as an inspiring, guiding and informing entity.

The 'Magic Square of Mars' is divided into 25 cells, or squares, five across and five down. The sum of the numbers in the vertical, horizontal and diagonal lines is a constant of 65. The total of these numbers is 325. Therefore, the numbers 5, 25, 65 and 325 are also assigned to Mars.

YOUR NUMEROLOGY NUMBER & LUCKY SUN SIGN NUMBERS

"Everything that exists has a vibration. The vibration of sound, music, colour, matter, even our words, thoughts, and names show form. All vibration is measurable. To measure we need numbers. Numbers are the basis of all. Numbers are the key to all mysteries."
Shirley Blackwell Lawrence, *Behind Numerology*

Numerology is essentially the metaphysical * 'science' of numbers. The use of numbers in magic is its cornerstone of power. The ancient Greek philosopher and mathematician Pythagoras, born around 590 BC, embarked on a thirty-year spiritual quest studying with important religious and esoteric teachers and healers to find the mystery of 'The Hidden Light', and came to see mankind as living in three worlds: the natural, the human and the Divine. He asserted that all things can be expressed in numerical terms, because they are ultimately reducible to numbers. Pythagoras stated that "Numbers are the first things of all of Nature" and followed the theory that "Nothing can exist without numbers."

Many believe that numbers have an arcane, mystical relationship with words, and with inanimate and animate objects; the interpretations that arose from these relationships date back to a time when the dawning intelligence of primitive man first visualised the meaning of numbers and associated it with spiritual significance. Numerology is the science of the exploration of this relationship in order to discover hidden meanings, forecast the future or interpret the character of a person. In its more modern applications, a series of figures which correspond to an individual's name and date of birth are calculated, and practitioners believe one's prospects, fortune and character can be deciphered from the results ^.

So what is numerology and how does one use it? Everything in the Universe has a vibrational frequency, an energy, a force, all vibrating at various rates, and we as humans are no exception, the difference between one person and another is their rate of vibration. This force or energy is constantly in motion and changing, and we can even 'tune into' and feel our vibrations if we are still for long enough.

Along with letters, sounds, colours, crystals, and many other things, it is believed that numbers also have vibrations, and when we are able to familiarise ourselves with our own numerical frequencies, we can use this familiarity to add power and magic to our lives. The numbers of our birth date, the letters of our names, and the numbers of our Sun sign and ruling planets, all have a unique vibrational frequency, and herein lies the key to understanding our self and our journey through life. Numerology refers to the knowledge contained within the numbers of our birth date and our name, and this is our own personal magic which can greatly assist us through life.

* Metaphysics is the study of those sciences that extend beyond the physical or tangible

HOW TO FIND YOUR NUMEROLOGY NUMBER

^ Your Sun sign's number was added up according to the principle of corresponding a number with a letter, for example 1=A, 2=B, 3=C and so on in sequence and up to 9=I, then beginning again at number 1 for the next letter J and following this same sequence. Following this system, the sum of the letters in Aries vibrates to the number 7.

Your personal numerology number is determined by adding up all the numbers in your birth date until they reach a two-digit figure. The two resulting numbers are then added together again to form a single digit, which is your personal numerology number. For example, someone born on 3 February 1983, would add the digits $3 + 2 + 1 + 9 + 8 + 3 = 26 =$ (reduced to two digits) 8. So that person's personal numerology birth number is 8.

Each primary number or birth number from 1 to 9 has a specific meaning and is governed by a planetary force. The principle of numerology reduces all numbers down to the following: 1 to 9, and 10, 11, 13 and 22 *. The last four numbers only apply to people specially concerned with the occult and spiritualism - and can be studied at greater length through other sources if so desired - and can in any case be reduced further to a single digit if preferred. Your birth number contains a unique power, and therein lie your strengths, shortcomings and opportunities. It is beyond the scope of this book to outline your individual numerology number possibilities, so for the purposes of astrological applications, I have only included your Sun sign and ruling planet's special numbers.

* The numbers 10 and 13, and the master numbers 11 and 22, can be further reduced to one digit if so desired; however, they can be interpreted as they are without further reduction. The choice is personal.

BASIC MEANINGS & KEYWORDS

1 ★ Sun. Masculine influence, beginnings, independence, inventiveness, originality, leadership, exploration, innovation, ambition

2 ★ Moon. Feminine influence, cooperation, partnership, tact, diplomacy, harmony, unity, emotions, imagination, adaptability

3 ★ Jupiter. Communication, expression, youthfulness, self-confidence, creativity, inspiration, optimism, curiosity

4 ★ Uranus. Order, form, security, stability, patience, restriction, work, values, practicality

5 ★ Mercury. Freedom, inconsistency, change, variety, travel, activity, learned

6 ★ Venus. Love, home, family, sense of duty, responsibility, marriage, justice, nurturing, balance, gentleness, peace, friendship

7 ★ Neptune. Analysis, wisdom, mystical, spiritual, solitude, precision, research, integrity, mystery, psychic perceptions

8 ★ Saturn. Money, power, success, organisation, hard work, business, health, purpose, control, authority, mastery

9 ★ Mars. Completion, endings, Universal, service, humanity, philanthropy, loyalty

10 ★ Fortunate, creative, vibrant, stable, optimistic, original, successful, determined, individualistic

11 ★ Master number. Prophecies, inspiration, moral courage, missionary, long-suffering, foolhardiness, enlightenment, invention

13 ★ Misunderstood, fearful, changeable, interested in the occult, fatalistic, flexible, sacred, beguiling

22 ★ Master number. Powerful, successful, idealistic, attracted to the occult, creative, wise, successful, masterful, spiritually understanding

★ THE NUMBER 9 - FOR MARS ★

Names ★ Novena, Ninth, Ennead, Enneagon, Nonagon

Arithmomantic connections with the letters of the alphabet ★ I and R

Ruled by Mars, 9 is a multiple of the lucky 3, so 9 is also a lucky number. The number 9 is usually regarded as second in significance only to number 3 among the odd numbers, primarily because it is the product of 3 by 3. It is sometimes considered the ultimate number, with special and even sacred significance. The Nonagon, the number 9, or the Ennead was known to many ancient cultures as Perfection and Concord, and as being unbounded.

Magicians of former times would draw a magic circle 9 feet in diameter, in which to practice their magic. It is the number of the Universe and of vision, representing spiritual ideals, philosophy and perfection.

Nine is the number of completion, bringing together all the creative forces to reach a conclusion. It is almost the most indestructible of the odd numbers in the sense that all its multiples reduce to nine if we add together the digits of which they are composed. Consequently, it is considered the number of ultimate achievement and without interruption, and along with the number 8, as the symbol of eternal life. Cats are thought to have nine lives and are often connected to witchcraft and other magical doctrines. Number 9 is a tolerant, impractical and sympathetic vibration.

Character ★ Number 9 symbolises the planet Mars, and its people are often fighters - active and determined, they usually succeed after a struggle, but they are also prone to accidents and injury, and may be quarrelsome. It signifies a jack-of-all-trades, generosity and heartiness on the one hand, but self-centeredness, arrogance, self-pity, fickleness, financial carelessness, moodiness, discontentment, restlessness, sullenness, mental instability and emotional volatility on the other. They are helpful, compassionate, active, determined, tolerant, emotional, sophisticated, generous, charitable, humanitarian, romantic, cooperative, creative, proud, self-sufficient and self-sacrificing.

Carrying the Martian vibe, those under its influence love all forms of art, drama and entertainment as well as being drawn to a deep interest in philosophy. These souls' doors are always open and there is always a pot of something boiling away on the stove. Perfect for artistic and philanthropic types, it is not so ideal for those who are more retiring. Number 9s are life's drama queens, there being rarely a dull moment around them, but they also stand for unconditional love, forgiveness and completion. With a great love of stage, food, movies and travel, they adore and immerse themselves in anything that resembles the broader canvas of life. The conception of perfection, concord and boundlessness, when applied to the human character, must necessarily be modified if you were born under this influence, for none of these traits, in their fullest sense, is human - they are all Divine.

Number 9 types will show great intelligence and a power of understanding and discretion. You will know how to use your knowledge effectively, however your chief interests will lie not so much in practical matters as in affairs of the intellect, in logic, philosophy and an appreciation of the fine arts. Success by sheer hard work or slogging is not for you; you become outstanding among your peers because of natural intellect and sheer inspiration. You make a good friend and never take advantage of others; you are always willing to help other people succeed, and make an excellent advisor because of your naturally sympathetic understanding. Like number 6, 9 inspires a lofty sense of morals, its subjects being strictly honest in all their thoughts and actions.

Frequently the number 9 is the number of the genius. Issues which may handicap or hinder your development are similar to those present in the number 6. Excessive dreaminess and too much value set on knowledge itself, apart from its application, may tend to cause lethargy and lack of progress. You should learn the value of hard work and concentration, otherwise there is a danger you may degenerate into a clever dabbler, without achieving outstanding success in any particular field. You are fortunate enough to be blessed with natural gifts, and should do all in your power to put these to the best purpose for benefiting both yourself and the world at large. At its best, number 9 will influence the highest qualities of courage, humanity, service and brotherhood. Number 9 people should try to carry out their plans on a Tuesday, the day governed by their planet, Mars.

Alchemy ★ Nine is a significant and magical number. It equals three times three, and in mythology, we often find an original trio who have expanded to nine. Each point of the triangle can generate another triangle. In this sense, nine has an essentially expansive, lively form of energy, that can include detail and diversity expanded from the basic three. Representations of nine usually combine the three triangles in some way. It represents completion - life flows in cycles of 9 - 9 years, 9 months, 9 days - and throughout life our major changes tend to happen with our personal 9 year. Numbers 1 to 9 are the basic vibrations and represent our 9 basic experiences of life. These experiences relate to our inner world and also to our outer world, and with a deeper understanding of the correlations between our experiences and the identifying numbers 1 to 9, we have an excellent reference for all aspects of our self and our journey through life.

LUCKY 'MAGIC HOURS' OR 'TIME UNITS'

One rule of magic, luck and power, as already outlined elsewhere in this book, can be found within the well-known phrase, "As above, so below." From the most ancient times, the planets were said to rule Earthly destinies and powers. Days of the week were named after the seven planets which were the only ones then known: Sun Day, Moon Day, Mars Day (French: Mardi), Mercury Day (French: Mercredi), Jove Day (French: Jeudi), Venus Day (French: Vendredi) and Saturn Day.

The planetary hours are based on an ancient astrological system, the Chaldean order of the planets. The Chaldean order indicates the relative orbital velocity of the planets, and from a heliocentric (helios = The Sun) perspective, this sequence also indicates the relative distance of the planets from the Sun (the Sun switching places with the Earth in this sequence), and the distance of the Moon from the Earth.

Before an action is taken in daily life, or a transaction undertaken, for instance, it is possible to choose the appropriate day and hour that will provide the greatest chances of success. By studying the planetary hours system, you will discover which actions are propitious to which of the seven planets or 'star-gods' and at what time it would be advisable to undertake them.

The planetary hours system uses this Chaldean order to divide time, and each planetary hour of the planetary day is ruled by a different planet. The order is repeated, starting with the slowest: Saturn - then, Jupiter, Mars, Sun, Venus, Mercury, Moon, then back to Saturn, Jupiter, Mars, etc, ad infinitum. The planet that rules the first hour of the day is also the ruler of that whole day and gives the day its name. So the first hour of Saturday is ruled by Saturn, the first hour of Sunday by the Sun, and so on. It is important, for the purposes of using specific planetary energies for our magic and wishes, to note that planetary hours are not considered the same length as our normal time-keeping slots of sixty minutes. Each day is split into time periods, day time and night time, beginning at around sunrise and sunset respectively. These two time periods are each divided into twelve equal-length hours, which are the planetary hours. So the planetary hours of the day and the planetary hours of the night will be of different lengths, except during the equinoxes when light and darkness are balanced.

In sequence, the Sun, Moon and the five visible planets each exerts its own special influence over a twenty-four-hour period. I like to call your planet's special day and hour the 'Magic Hour'.

Magic rituals to draw luck and love to you should be conducted at astrologically correct times and with the appropriate instruments, tools, cards, herbs, flowers, oils and plants which are linked with the ruling planet. For example, a love ritual, spell or potion demands a concoction of any or all of the above ruled by Venus. Do not underestimate rulerships, for they wield an unseen power that can help make our dreams, big and small, come true.

Further, as specific hours of each day are ruled by certain planets, if you are really serious about attracting some power, luck or magic into your life, it is imperative that you wish, pray or ask at the most opportune times for your Sun sign. There are two methods you can use for fine tuning your magical workings. The first method is to perform your spell, ritual or wishing on the day your Sun sign's ruling planet during the planetary hour that signifies the essence of what you are asking for (e.g. An Arien who is looking for love might perform a love-seeking ritual on a Tuesday, during a Venus-ruled planetary hour). Alternatively, if you wish to summon the power of your Sun sign's own ruling planet, then that same Arien might perform their love-seeking ritual on a Friday (ruled by Venus) during Mars's planetary hour.

The nature of that which you are asking for, such as love, travel opportunities, money, career guidance, protection or friendship for example, should always be considered when choosing the day or hour during which your magic will be heightened.

The answer to the question why are there seven days in a week, is a very important one to know in unravelling the secret of your Magic Hours. Ancient people recognised the supreme importance of the seven heavenly spheres, which comprised those which could be seen by the naked eye: The Sun, Moon, Mercury, Venus, Mars, Jupiter and Saturn. They then named each of the seven days of the week after one of those spheres and assigned that planetary 'ruler' to one day of the week. As viewed from Earth, these seven spheres appear to move at varying speeds, and the ancients used this factor to arrange them in order of varying speed. If you intend to use your Magic Hours to attract wonderful things, you must memorise that sequence because it is what forms the basis of the whole system.

Whenever you intend to use your Magic Hours or, perhaps more accurately, Magic *Time Units*, it is important to find out the exact time of sunrise for the area in which you live, as sunrise marks the time when your planet's magic is at its most powerful on its specific day. So, at sunrise on Sunday, the Sun rules the hour following the sunrise, the Moon rules the first hour following sunrise on a Monday, and through the week the pattern is repeated, with each day's ruling planet beginning the cycle in that first hour after dawn. It is logical then, that the rest of the planets, in sequence, follow on with one planet per hour for that day thereafter for the rest of the 24-hour cycle, creating a Magic Hour or Time Unit for each planet throughout the day and night, depending on which planet rules that particular day and is therefore the first in line.

If you wish to explore the idea in more depth, it is worth noting first and foremost that each day contains twenty-four hours, but, depending on the season, day and night will be of varying lengths. In summer, daylight is longer than darkness, whereas the reverse applies in winter. During autumn and spring, day and night are usually about equal. Therefore, although a complete day always contains twenty-four hours, there are not always twelve hours between sunrise and sunset and another twelve hours between sundown and the following sunrise. So, depending on the season (and location), a time unit may be shorter than one hour, longer than one hour, or equal to one hour. So whenever you intend to use your Magic Time Units, it is important to find out the exact time of sunrise and sunset for the area in which you live. The next step is to divide the amount of day time (if day when you wish to work your 'magic', otherwise the same following theory applies to night time) into twelve equal sections by calculating the number of hours and minutes between sunrise and sunset and divide by twelve. An example is if the Sun rises at 6.27 a.m. and sets at 5.49 p.m., the amount of time contained in this day is eleven hours and twenty-two minutes. Convert this total into minutes (682) and then divide that figure by twelve (57). Therefore, each of the twelve daylight time units will be 57 minutes on that day.

Although this wonderful method of using astrology is very ancient, it may be completely new to you. You are in for a pleasant surprise though, because if you are willing to delve into a little research and put the system to the test, rich rewards are in store for you!

YOUR LUCKY DAY ★ TUESDAY

Planet ★ Mars
Basic Energy ★ Action
Basic Magic ★ Combat, Courage, Vitality, Willpower
Element ★ Fire
Colour ★ Red
Energy Keywords ★ Assertion, Force, Frankness, Will, Passion, Expression, Leadership, Construction, Courage, Strength, Defiance, Combat, Destruction, Dynamism, Audacity, Energy, Self-reliance, Fearlessness, Heroics, Impulsivity, Spontaneity

Tuesday is the day of Mars, your ruler. In commonly used calendars, Tuesday is the third day of the week, though in others it is the second. The English name is derived from Old English *Tiwesdaeg*, and Middle English *Tewesday*, meaning 'Tiw's Day', the Day of Tiw or Tyr, the god of victory, war, combat and heroic glory in Norse mythology. Tiw was equated with Mars. Shrove Tuesday, which precedes the first day of Lent in the Western Christian calendar, and Black Tuesday, referring to Tuesday 29 October 1929, part of the Great Stock Market Crash of that year, are two famous days with which Mars's day is associated.

In the folk rhyme 'Monday's Child', ' Tuesday's child is full of grace'. Tuesday offers Mars energy to end conflicts, to overcome inertia or to deal with those matters that may metaphorically need to be kick-started, or have physical energy applied to them.

It can be a day of passionate feelings, strong motivations and determined efforts that bring desired results.

Tuesday is a day of Enthusiasm, Competition, Passion, Energy, Courage, Protection, Strength, Victory, Anything Requiring Assertiveness, Masculinity (Yang Energy), Standing up for Yourself, a 'Fighting Spirit', Determination, Vitality, Sexuality, Virility, Self-confidence, Men's Power, Men's Mysteries, Drive, Ambition, Achievement, Triumph and Potency.

MARS'S MAGIC TIME UNITS
(BASED ON THE PLANETARY HOURS)
FOR EACH DAY OF THE WEEK

SATURDAY ★ Third and Tenth time units after sunrise
SUNDAY ★ Seventh time unit after sunrise
MONDAY ★ Fourth and Eleventh time units after sunrise
TUESDAY ★ First and Eighth time units after sunrise
WEDNESDAY ★ Fifth and Twelfth time units after sunrise
THURSDAY ★ Second and Ninth time units after sunrise
FRIDAY ★ Sixth time unit after sunrise **

Choose the Hour/s of Mars for any transaction, activity, exchange, initiative or venture which involves sport, winning, overcoming enemies, conquering, overthrowing enemies, self-mastery, bravery, combating, calling one into battle, gaining courage, resolving quarrels, being more decisive, and taking action in any given situation.

** Please note that for the purposes of simplification, the information regarding 'Mars's Magic Time Units' is a very diluted and simplified version of using magical times to your advantage. These hours cover only daylight hours, or the first twelve hours after sunrise, and do not take into account magical times after sunset or throughout the night. 'Hours' is also a deceptive term, as most 'time periods' used in this system are less than an hour, but for the purposes of simplifying the technique, I refer to them as Magic Hours (to keep with the tradition of the term 'planetary hours') rather than magic 'time units', which is what they really are. Should you wish to do further research on your ruling planet's most powerful time units, or require further information about the planet/s from which you are seeking 'energy' from in order to assist your wish-making, other sources may provide you with more comprehensive and detailed information.

A LITTLE NEW MOON / MAGICAL TIME UNIT WISH RITUAL

Step 1 ~ Choose the Magical Hour and/or day that matches your intentions. The first dawn hour of Sunday, ruled by the Sun, is a great time for all-purpose magic, success, joy, abundance, prosperity, bliss, personal power & all-round expansion.

Step 2 ~ Write out a little wish list with the appropriate coloured pen on the colour paper which corresponds to your desire.

Step 3 ~ Choose a small stone of your choosing that is connected to your wish (or a number of stones, that are perhaps linked with your planetary ruler's number, for example 9 for Mars).

Step 4 ~ Find a nice patch of soil in your garden or any special place to you, dig into it, affirm your wish in your mind, place the crystal/s and piece of paper in the hole, then place a plant on top of the crystal/s and wish list.

Step 5 ~ Fill the soil back in over the roots of the plant and feed it with a little water out of a magical vessel (a small genie bottle would be ideal).

Step 6 ~ Thank the Earth, the Universe and the Sun (or whatever planet you are summoning the power from) for bringing forth your desires.

Step 7 ~ Repeat all day long: "Thank You, Thank You, Thank You!"

Step 8 ~ Watch your plant - and your wish - grow bigger and bigger as time goes on!

YOUR LUCKY CHARM/TALISMANS

The following are three 'materials' or talismanic symbols from which to make your lucky charms, and the planetary energy under which to do it, corresponding with your Sun sign:

ARIES ★ Diamond, Axe, Iron, Mars

"When any star ascends fortunately, take a stone and
herb that are under that star, make a ring of
the metal that is congruous therewith, and in that fix
the stone with the herb under it."
Henry Cornelius Agrippa, *On Occult Philosophy*

Charms, talismans and amulets are among the oldest forms of magic. A charm or talisman is a symbol, often used to communicate a thought, prayer or wish to, or to make a connection with the Divine. It is usually in the form of an object, which has been imbued with mysterious and magical powers. A charm may be as simple as a stone, a flower or a feather, or it might be a parchment bearing writing; the meaning and significance that you attribute to the symbol is what is important. It can be created by yourself (to best effect) or by someone else, and works as a tool to activate our subconscious mind.

You can use general charms such as a cross, or a universally lucky symbol such as a horseshoe, but you will exude and therefore attract more potency and protection if you make and wear the appropriate charms with the matching gemstone, set in the right metal and created under the corresponding planetary influence. While most people wear silver or gold, cheaper tin or copper may be more appropriate and indeed beneficial for your Sun sign. An amulet (for protection) or a talisman or charm (for luck), must also be made, ordered, designed or purchased on the appropriate day of the week for its power to be most effective. Your day, as previously described, is Tuesday.

You can even go further and create or buy your amulet or charm at one of the hours and/or days when your planet is exerting its most powerful influence. It may sound complicated and requiring of forethought and effort, but if you are going to summon magic and are superstitious enough to truly *believe* that you can do this (and remember pure belief in something is the starting point of all manifestation), you should be scrupulous enough to do it properly. For your planet's day and time, please consult the information under the previous headings 'Your Lucky Day' and 'Mars's Magic Time Units'.

GODS, GODDESSES, ANIMAL TOTEMS & OTHER 'GUIDES'

Gods, goddesses and guides can be summoned to help you live your life to its optimal best. Some are connected with your Sun sign, while others may be of your own personal choosing, ones you may feel particularly drawn towards. Those which align with your ruling planet and your Sun sign, give a good indication of those who will shine a guiding light along your desired path, but you can choose your own too, based upon exploration, observations, research, meditation or simple intuition - I believe choosing your own, based on your inner *knowing* or guidance system, is a very powerful magical tool. However, to get you started, following are some animal spirit guide ideas for your contemplation. Good luck!

YOUR LUCKY ANIMALS & BIRDS

Ram, Dragon, Falcon, Tiger, Leopard, Magpie,
Stallion, Vulture, Robin, Hawk

"Somewhere beyond the walls of our awareness …
the wilderness side, the hunter side, the seeking side
of ourselves is waiting to return."
Laurens van der Post, *The Heart of the Hunter*

"(People) everywhere are being made acutely aware of
the fact that something essentially to life and
wellbeing is flickering very low in the human species
and threatening to go out entirely. This 'something'
has to do with such values as love, unselfishness,
sincerity, loyalty to one's best friend, honesty,
enthusiasm, humility, goodness, happiness … fun.
Practically every animal has these assets in abundance
and is eager to share them, given the opportunity and
the encouragement."
Jay Allen Boone, *Kinship with All Life*

Some astrological systems, such as Shamanistic *
or Native American Astrology, tell us that the Sun
sign we were born under has a corresponding animal
totem, which informs us about our characteristics and
act as a kind of spiritual guide or mentor throughout
our life's journey. These totems are described as Solar
totems, because many of them share similarities with
the Solar system and the sign the Sun was passing
through at the time of our birth, and therefore relate
to animals and animal behaviours which also
correspond to environmental conditions and seasonal

changes. These animals encompass many aspects of the Solar system, from seasonal relationships, to creature instincts, to reciprocal links with the planetary vibrations, and 'clans' within nature that you are inherently closely connected with through your date of birth.

Carl Jung, a master of dream analysis and interpretation, proposed that animals symbolise our natural instincts, operating through our dreams. He theorised that certain dream symbols, among them animals, represent core emotions and concepts, archetypes that will hold true for all of us the world over, regardless of so-called 'divisions' such as sex, customs, age or culture. In *Man and His Symbols*, Jung states that primitive societies believed that each person had a bush soul and a human soul. The bush soul incarnates as a tree or animal - a totem - and when the bush soul is harmed or injured, the human soul is considered injured as well.

Some of the most important and powerful spirit guides are those belonging to the animal kingdom. Both in ancient times and in some traditional modern tribal systems, people consult with animals for their wisdom and personal power. Even though most societies today have drifted away from this connection, it has never really left us, and different creatures continue to communicate with us on both the physical and spiritual planes in an attempt to speak to our souls and spirits.

As part of the teaching world, animals can bring us wisdom and survival skills, while others show us how to adapt, transcend or morph. Others still can remind us the importance of play and humour, and guide us around how to overcome life's challenges. Many are known for their loyalty and ability to love unconditionally and without judgement, while some have a grounded and healthy detachment, remaining true to themselves rather than pleasing others, an important lesson in itself. Whatever the qualities of the unique animal guides for your Sun sign, all have some enlightening soul-awakening traits that can teach us much about our own true inner selves. Ultimately, your animal spirit guides, and in particular your Solar totem animal, endow you with qualities that will enhance your life and help to activate your creativity, wisdom and intuition, helping to heal the broken or return the lost pieces of your soul and reconnect you to the natural world.

Your Solar totem animal (listed last on your lucky birds and animals list) is not the same as an animal spirit guide, which is based on metaphysical principles and is also based on your soul's mission in this embodiment - however, you can definitely make your birth Solar totem animal your spiritual guide if you wish, as you may find that its qualities, traits, symbolism and messages strongly reflect and define your own nature - or what you aspire to become, manifest or draw towards you. Your birth totem power animal comes from a place of trust and innocence, and represents the essence of your creative inner child. If you spend some time meditating on your Solar totem animal, asking what lessons it can teach, and reflect deeply on its character, life and habits, you may find it connects with you on a deep spiritual level and you can make the necessary changes to your life to draw in more magic and power.

Overall, if your life is stagnant or in need of healing or an energy boost, you can request your animal spirit or spirits to come and help you change your vibration, awaken your truth and arouse your inner forces. If you are aware of your animal spirit's presence in your life every day, you can use its particular energies to support, guide and teach you. And above all, pay attention to any signs and expressions of its lessons, and remember to thank your chosen animal guide for helping you.

* Shamanism is a traditional spiritual practice of the Native American culture. A shaman, one who practices this age-old art, is an intermediary between the human world and the world of the spirits. He inherits his magical powers at birth, but spends many years as an apprentice, so that he is usually much older in age before he is able to practice and call upon his skills. People ask for a shaman's help when there is a crisis on either a personal or wider spread scale, such as famine, drought, war or illness. The shaman makes contact with the spirits by going into a trance. First, he may perform a series of rituals, which usually include drumming, singing and chanting, and when these have brought on the right conditions, he leaves his body behind to travel to the other world. There he meets with the spirits of his ancestors, who inform him what must be done to relieve the suffering of his people. If the shaman is asked to cure someone of a dis-ease, then the spirits may accompany him to find the correct medicinal herbs or treatments for his patient.

YOUR FEATURE ANIMAL ★ RED HAWK

The Hawk's Message ★ Strike while the iron is hot
Brings the totem gift of ★ Initiative, courage, leadership, discernment
Shares the power energies of ★ Achievement, action, opportunity, wisdom, truth
Brings forth and teaches the magic of ★ Passion, Fire, confidence, persistence, observation

The Hawk is the great communicator, giving reason to the conversations in our head, and expression to our ideas. A natural born leader, the Hawk has initiative and always takes action while the time is ripe. Ever persistent and a little bit arrogant at times, the cockiness can be forgiven with the knowledge that their opinions are usually the right ones. The Hawk soars in his or her ability to maintain the passion and Fire, and a little impatience from time to time will usually provide the drive needed to get things done.

The Hawk's gifts include clear-sightedness, long-term memory, messages from the Universe, being observant, guardianship, memories from past lives, courage, illumination, seeing the bigger picture, creativity, wise use of opportunities, the 'truth', magic, focus and overcoming problems.

Associated with the number 14 and the Tarot card, Temperance, it represents the embracing of higher expressions of vision and psychic abilities.

Hawks are the supreme flyers, protectors and visionaries of the Air, holding the key to higher levels of consciousness. This power animal has the potential to inspire vision and awaken you to your creative life purpose.

The Red-tailed Hawk is especially powerful and it will always be with you, Aries, for life. Having direct ties to the kundalini (life force) and links to the Base chakra, it is the seat of the primal force. With the Hawk as your power animal, you have a responsibility to recognise and work towards fulfilling your soul's destiny; and you will be especially aware of omens and spirit messages that draw you towards this. It reflects a great intensity of energy at work in your life, and you will feel these spiritual forces strongly.

All Hawks share the ability to move gracefully between the seen and unseen realms, joining both worlds together. The Hawk also endows you with acute and broad vision, which keep you out of danger's way, and allows you to see into the future; in this way it stands as a symbol of prophetic insight.

In Native American culture, the Hawk stands for messenger, and it will often show up in our lives in some form if something requires our attention or focus. As with all messages received, it is important to undercover the underlying meanings, and through this we will learn to become more observant and pay attention to that which we may overlook. This could mean an untapped talent, a gift or some unexpected help for which we haven't shown gratitude, or even a message from the wider Universe. As there are so many Hawk varieties, their messages can vary and can affect all and different levels of our psyches. Therefore, the personal qualities of discernment and discrimination are important when deciphering your totem bird's code.

The Hawk denotes All That Is. It is truly a bird of the heavens, arranging circumstances and conditions necessary to prompt our spiritual growth.

You may ignore the Hawk chasing you, or dodge him for a time, but you can never fully escape your ultimate destiny, and when the Hawk gets hold of us in his powerful talons, we will be asked to evaluate who we really are, what we are trying to escape from, destroy our self-created illusions, and invite our inner self out to shine in the light of the truth. After all, having this animal as your totem can be a bittersweet experience, for through accepting its presence in your life, you will be asked to surrender anything that doesn't honour integrity in your life. From the powerful, all-seeing Hawk, you can certainly run, but you can never truly hide.

SPIRITUAL KEEPER ★ EAGLE

Your spiritual keeper guides your spiritual growth and brings illumination. Your spiritual keeper is determined by the season in which you were born. Regarded as the 'keepers' or 'caretakers' of the Universe, the four Directions or alignments were also referred to by the Native Americans as the Four Winds because their presence was *felt* rather than seen. The Direction to which your birth time belongs influences the nature of your inner senses. The East Direction's totem is the Eagle.

The Eagle is a symbol of freedom, victory and spirit. It flies higher than any other bird, high enough to 'touch the Sun'. The golden Eagle is a symbol of peace, and an Eagle flying overhead is a sign of Shaman power, sometimes taken as a call to that vocation. To the shaman, the Eagle is a messenger, bringing instructions from the spirit of the night. As Halifax states, "When shamans get power, it always comes from the night." The Eagle is the sacred messenger, flying high to carry our prayers to the Great Spirit and returning with gifts of illumination and clear vision. The Eagle enables us to see the bigger picture, to rise above our Earthly concerns, and reminds us to pay attention to the things that really matter in life. This majestic bird brings you the totem gift of freedom, mission and perfect timing, sharing the power energies and magic of pride, spirit and manifestation. Your animal keeper the Eagle is, above all, a potent symbol of vision and strength.

CLAN ★ THUNDERBIRD (OR HAWK)

Your clan animal comes from a place of inner knowing and intuition, helping you to discover the essence and magic of your true self. The Thunderbird, sometimes referred to as Hawk, is a Totem of the Fire clan, and its medicine is messenger. Thunderbird holds the Fire clan and brings thunder, lightning and rain. The greatest of all the winged creatures, the Thunderbird is closest to the Creator. His Fire and spark carry the gift of life and link the soul to the Great Mystery.

Thunderbird people are doers, often leaders, and are usually found in the spotlight expressing their feelings. Naturally invigorated by thunder and lightning, Thunderbird clan people are energised by the air just before and after a storm. Ever seeking a higher union with Spirit, Thunderbird souls have a responsibility to all the aspects of their element - Fire, Sun and lightning - and it is important for them to understand the power and purpose of these things. As trailblazers of the other three clans, they are born with the drive to initiate and to function within the greater tribe of Humanity, progressing it by broadening boundaries. You are not travelling the Great Road to build or to harvest, but rather you are forging the way ahead in preparation for the planting and harvesting that will be done by the other clans.

The challenge for the Thunderbird clan is to learn the virtues of patience, for to effectively utilise our natural gifts we must also be aware of our polar opposites - and integrate the two to create a meaningful input that yields fulfilment and results for the benefit of ourselves and others. Visualise the Thunderbird/Hawk in your spirit to be soaring high and being held aloft by the invisible hands of the Four Winds. Your eyes scan all before you and above you, and your keen perception is without equal. The Thunderbird's true desire is not to know what lies below; your true yearning is to join with Grandfather Sky. Fly high and keep your eyes focused ever upward.

YOUR CORRESPONDING CHINESE ASTROLOGY ANIMAL

The Chinese Zodiac, known as Sheng Xiao (literally meaning 'birth likeness'), is based on a twelve-year cycle, each year in that cycle related to a particular animal. These animals are: Rat, Ox, Tiger, Rabbit, Dragon, Snake, Horse, Sheep, Monkey, Rooster, Dog and Pig. The selection and order of the animals that so influence people's lives, particularly in East Asian cultures, originated in the Han Dynasty (202 BC - 220 AD) and was based upon each animal's traits, characteristics, tendencies and living habits. Further, ancient people observed that there were twelve Full Moons in a year, and that, among other similarly related celestial observations, suggests its origins are also based on astronomical concepts.

The legend of the Chinese zodiac's story usually begins with the Jade Emperor, or Buddha (depending on who is telling the tale), summoning all the animals of the Universe for a race or a banquet. The twelve animals of the zodiac all appeared at the palace, and the order in which they arrived determined the order of the Chinese zodiac.

Each oriental animal corresponds with a Western astrology sign. For Aries, it is the Dragon.

> "I am an unquenchable fire,
> The centre of all energy,
> The stout heroic heart.
> I am truth and light,
> I hold power and glory in my sway.

My presence
Disperses dark clouds.
I have been chosen
To tame the Fates.
I am the Dragon."
Theodora Lau

Chinese name for the Dragon ★ LONG
Ranking Order ★ Fifth
Hours ruled by the Dragon ★ 7 a.m. to 9 a.m.
Direction ★ East - Southeast
Season and principle month ★ Spring - April
Corresponds to the Western sign ★ Aries

★ **DRAGON** ★ Fixed Element Wood

★ **Keywords** ★
Honourable, Excitable, Healthy, Inflexible, Brave,
Intelligent, Independent, Enthusiastic, Flamboyant,
Vital, Energetic, Short-tempered, Proud

"I know that the birds can fly, I know that the fishes
can swim, I know that the wild animals can run.
For the running, one could make nooses; for the
swimming, one could make nets; for the flying, one
could make arrows. As to the dragon I cannot know
how he can bestride wind and clouds when
he rises heavenward. Today I saw Lao Tzu. Is he
perhaps the dragon?"
**Confucius, on Lao Tzu (author of the Tao Te Ching,
the 'Book of the Way')**

The Dragon is the fifth animal of the Chinese horoscope. Traditionally a yang animal, the Dragon is a mythical creature who endows qualities of self-sufficiency, wildness, sentimentality and shrewdness. They are vibrant characters, but tend to be judgemental towards others. As the noble animal symbol that represents the Chinese emperors, Dragons are born leaders and masters of ceremonies, and because of this, many Chinese parents aspire to have a Dragon child. Feisty and gifted with power and luck, many look up to the Dragon type, but the Dragon can be enthusiastic and proud to the point of impetuosity, losing their tempers easily. Dragons can be tyrannical and grab at prestige and splendour, but they are also generous, gifted, tenacious, willing and intelligent. Dragons are born monarchs, and as far as they can see, their power is indisputable and unconquerable - and for this reason they are usually successful in all they undertake.

YOUR METALS

Arien power metals are Iron and Steel.

Although the magic power of crystals is widely recognised and applied, the influence radiating from metals is often overlooked. Metal, too, emits a powerful energy and in fact, in Chinese philosophy, metal is considered so essential and powerful that it is classified as one of the elements, alongside Air, Fire, Earth and Water.

As already mentioned earlier in the book, throughout the writings of early philosophers and theorists, there are countless references to the unmistakable mystic connection between the seven known planets of the time, and Earthly affairs, ailments and objects. Seven metals were connected with the seven planets, to which seven colours and the seven 'transformations' were added. So the ancient alchemist came to share the astrological doctrine that each planet ruled a mineral: The Sun ruled gold, the Moon silver, Mars iron, Venus copper, Saturn lead, Jupiter tin, and Mercury quicksilver. Consequently, in alchemical symbolism the same sign came to represent the nominated metal and its corresponding planet.

IRON & STEEL

"His metal is iron, and its unbendable strength gives him nine times as many lives to live as others; nine times as many chances of winning the battle."
Linda Goodman

Iron is a chemical element with symbol Fe (from Latin *ferrum*). By mass it is the most common element on Earth, forming much of our planet's inner and outer core. The symbol for Mars, your ruler, has been used since antiquity to represent the element iron.

Iron is the metal most associated with magic. Although not glistening or beautiful like silver or gold, at times in history iron's value was considered superior. Because iron is not found in its pure state except as a meteorite, it was known as the 'Metal of Heaven'. Iron's celestial origins were recognised early in human history and meteorites were perceived as supreme conduits to the spiritual realm. Iron is known for its protective and healing capacities; iron boxes serve to safeguard their contents, keeping their powers intact, and an iron bed is thought to be psychically protective, enhance one's dreaming processes and even promotes physical healing. These protective qualities are well-known and iron amulets are said to also guard and protect children and newborns. As well, because iron is connected with virility and fertility, an iron bed and iron jewellery are considered auspicious for romance and conception.

The metal iron has been used since ancient times, and is relatively soft but significantly hardened and strengthened by impurities, particularly carbon (a certain proportion of present carbon will produce steel, which can be up to a thousand times harder than pure iron). The first production of iron began in the Middle Bronze Age, but it was several centuries before iron displaced bronze. Iron of meteoric origin was highly regarded due to its origins in the heavens, and was often used to forge weapons and tools, having a distinct advantage over bronze in warfare instruments, as it is much harder and more durable than bronze (albeit more susceptible to rust).

In more modern times, steels and iron alloys are the most common metals used in industry, due to their vast range of desirable properties and Earth's widespread abundance of iron-bearing rock. It is the most widely used of all the metals, accounting for over 90 per cent of worldwide metal production. Its low cost and high strength make it invaluable in many engineering applications, such as the construction of machinery, mechanical tools, the hulls of large ships, automobiles and the structural components of buildings. And since it is in its pure state quite soft, it is the most commonly combined with alloying metals to create steel. This industrial iron production begins with iron ores, principally hematite and magnetite, two of your 'lucky stones'.

Iron also plays a vital role in biology - iron proteins are found in all living organisms - forming complexes with molecular oxygen in haemoglobin and myoglobin, and in the functioning of various enzymes, cellular respiration, and oxidation and reduction in animals and plants.

The word iron, when used metaphorically, refers to certain traits of the metal. Used as an adjective and sometimes as a noun, it can refer to something that is sturdy, unyielding, stern, unbreakable, harsh, strong, formidable and robust. The 'Iron Lady' Margaret Thatcher was so named because of her 'iron-fisted' style of rulership.

Iron may be etched with hydraulic acid, or engraved. Iron is primarily used for healing when you feel under attack, and is believed to increase physical strength. Steel is sometimes used as an alternative.

Overall, iron has a number of good and not-so-good associations. The earliest specimens of iron were found in meteorites and it was highly prized among the Aztecs who regarded it as a metal sent from the gods. However, at the beginning of the Iron Age, smelted iron had evil connotations, and it was considered inferior to the other metals such as gold, copper and bronze. Although it is a metal usually linked with brute strength and masculinity, it has been adopted as a symbol of fertility; in folklore, wearing a bracelet made of iron is said to help with conceiving a child. In some countries, people would touch iron to bring them good luck. It certainly couldn't hurt to try.

PLANTS, HERBS, SPICES, TREES, SHRUBS, FLOWERS, SCENTS & INCENSE

Plants have long been associated with magic, medicinal properties, superstition, nutrition and even astrology. In ancient times, some were endowed with magical properties based upon beliefs of the time, but also upon anecdotal evidence that some herbal concoctions, flowers or essences helped alleviate and even cure uncomfortable, painful or dis-eased physical or mental states. Whether these were based upon 'old wives' tales' or beliefs in supernatural forces matters little, for in modern times we can prove and indeed *have* proven through scientific research and controlled experiments, that plants have their place in our health and medicine cabinets. Some 'magical' plants have aphrodisiac or narcotic properties, while others have formidable toxic effects, but all are considered in some way to affect the human system on physical, spiritual and psychological levels. Plants such as cocoa, tobacco and coffee, which have accompanied humans over the course of millennia, are still, more than ever, an integral part of our daily lives. They still incite the same pleasures, the same fascinations, and the same dangers, and some still carry the same taboos. It is interesting to note that more than 80 per cent of chemical medicines in existence today, and found in pharmacists' dispensaries, are made from plants.

In modern astrology herbs are often associated with the zodiac signs and have evolved from an old system where a specific planet rules each herb. The planet that governs a herb is chosen according to its appearance, scent and where it grows; herbs are additionally categorised as hot or cold, and dry or moist. In this way you can see how the nature of the herb corresponds to the nature of the planet. If you are familiar with your ruling planets' basic associations, you will find it easy to match it to herbs. Although you can simply buy whatever herbs you wish to use for your magic, the optimum effect will be obtained if you can gather them at a favourable astrological time. Once you are armed with astrological knowledge, you can choose a time when the planet that rules your chosen herb is in a position of strength. Keep in mind that each planet rules a substantial amount of plants, so if one isn't easily obtained, it should be simply to find another one to use for the same purpose.

There sometimes seems to be a wide variance in the list of herbs associated with a specific astrological influence. This is because the different parts of the plant have different rulerships and uses. For example, whichever planet rules it, a plant that bears fruit is naturally related to Jupiter, its flowers relate to Venus, seed or bark to Mercury, leaves to the Moon, wood to Mars, and roots to Saturn. So, as well as the planet that traditionally rules the plant, it can be regarded as having a secondary ruler according to the part of the plant being used. Although you don't need to work with a highly complex system of deciding which herb will suit your purposes, you can make your magical workings more powerful by paying attention to some of these nuances.

Essentially, different scents, herbs, flowers and plants have their own specific vibrations. Their essences should be worn on your skin (you can make up your own combinations using essential oils or flower waters), burned in an oil burner, inhaled from a cloth, diffused in a bath or bowl of steam, or burned as incense sticks. Many plants, herbs and spices, however used, contain gentle yet effective energies which will affect not only your wishing ceremonies, but also your moods, associations and emotions, which can assist in carrying your wonderful Self in the direction of your dreams. Lifted up on incense smoke, for example, your wish is carried out to the wider Universe. Try making your own, out of any or all of your power plants, woods, flowers, shrubs, trees or herbs!

Thirty-three magical, mythical plants are: Cocoa, rosemary, tobacco, thyme, wheat, coffee, sugar cane, cinnamon, hemp, tea, pumpkin, foxglove, incense, amanita (a mushroom), tarragon, pepper, rice, belladonna, reed, ginseng, clove, ginger, sage, maize, mistletoe, lily, mandrake, St John's Wort, poppy, peyote, cinchona, verbena and the vine *.

How many of your Arien 'lucky plants' (listed under the next sub-category, 'Your Lucky Plants, Herbs, Spices', etc.) can be found on this Magical 33 List?

YOUR LUCKY PLANTS, HERBS, SPICES, TREES, SHRUBS, FLOWERS, SCENTS, OILS & INCENSE

Chilli Peppers, Thistle, Daffodil, Yarrow, Centaury, Hawthorn, Fir, Gentian, Witch Hazel, Sweet Pea, Sassafras, Holly, Capers, Fo Ti, Peppermint, Hops, Salad Burnet, Heather, Chamomile, Geranium, Daisy, Rosemary, Chestnut, Blessed Thistle, Spruce, Nettle, Burdock Root, Yellow Dock, Poppy, Red Clover, Gotu Cola, Golden Broom, Honeysuckle, Marjoram, Garlic, Mustard, Horseradish, Impatiens, Cowslip Wine, Geranium, St John's Wort, Bryony, Fern, Anemone, and all thorn-bearing trees and shrubs. *

For Mars ★ Onion, Garlic, Nettle, Mustard, Cayenne, Holly. Mars is the planet of assertiveness, and plants associated with it are often red in colour and have thorns. Barberry Berries, Hawthorn & Sarsparilla are connected with Mars *

* Some plant products can be poisonous, toxic, hallucinogenic or even fatal if consumed. Always research first.

YOUR SPECIAL POWER FLOWERS

ARIES IN GENERAL ★ Honeysuckle

OTHER BIRTH FLOWERS ★ Gorse, Nasturtium, Thistle & Peppermint

MARCH BORN ★ Daffodil ★ The spiritually uplifting daffodil bestows dignity and chivalry on those born in March, the earliest month of the northern Hemisphere's springtime during which it first blooms. The daffodil has always been considered a cheerful flower that raises the spirits.

APRIL BORN ★ Sweet Pea ★ Together with grace and a sense of delicacy, the sweet pea brings with it the possibility of a varied life for the versatile April-born.

YOUR FOODS

Strident, confrontational, fiery, outdoorsy Aries types don't like parlous games or cool mushy foods. Aries tastes head south of the border. Your ruling planet Mars rules the colour red and is associated with heat and Fire. Being instinctive and primal, it was probably an Arien who coined the phrase "Give the man meat". Mars-ruled Ariens of both genders enjoy dense, sustaining pleasures of the flesh - both in the bedroom and on the dinner table. Being naturally active, you often eat on the run, and being hot-blooded, you would prefer a hot roast dinner over cold salads. Adventurous and a bit of a daredevil, you are likely to take up the challenge of eating exotic and out-there foods, such as Scottish haggis, tripe, black pudding, fried spiders, escargot (snails), Dragon in the Flame of Desire (a.k.a. yaks' penis) and anything eye-poppingly hot and spicy; the more novel and adventurous the dish, the more appealing you will find it! Bland, slow-cooked, repetitive or tedious are definitely not on the menu for the Ram.

ARIES POWER FOODS

"Let food be your medicine; let medicine be your food."
Hippocrates

Hot, dry and spicy foods, mustard, chillies, cayenne, curry, horseradish, black or white pepper, capers, anything strong-tasting are associated with

Aries. Onions, garlic, leeks, marjoram, oregano, watercress, spinach, hops, pungent foods, red foods, meat, red vegetables (red cabbage, red onions, red capsicum, radishes), red fruits (cranberries, redcurrants, cherries, strawberries, rhubarb, plums, ripe red tomatoes). Your power beverages are Coffee, Moonshine (do your research first!), Soda Pops, Bloody Mary, Alco Pops, Beer and, you guessed it, Red Wine. *

* Caution: Always use essential oils, alcohol and/or herbs with caution and research each one prior to use, as not all are safe for use by certain people, or under certain conditions such as pregnancy, intoxication or illness. Some herbs and oils may be hallucinogenic, toxic in high doses, or produce other undesirable effects, and may be considered potentially harmful or hazardous if used or consumed before operating machinery, driving, or combined with alcohol or other drugs. Always consult a qualified practitioner or undertake thorough research from reliable sources before use or consumption of any of the listed essential oils, herbs or foods.

YOUR LUCKY WOOD ★ MAHOGANY
(Great to make a magic wand out of!)

Native Americans referred to trees as 'Standing People' because they stand firm, obtaining strength from their connection with the Earth. They therefore teach us the importance of being grounded, while at the same time listening to, and reaching towards, our higher aspirations. In Norse mythology, Yggdrasil, the tree of life, is a cosmic map that represents all life. The tree has its roots in the Underworld, is linked to the Earth through its trunk and its branches reach into the air of the Otherworld of spirit. The dryad, or tree's spirit, needs to be respected and asked when 'taking' from a tree for the purposes of magic.

The essence of tree magic lies in understanding the qualities of each type. These can be drawn on for such things as healing and spell-casting. For example, the rowan tree grows high up the sides of mountains, often in hard-to-reach places, so if you need to develop tenacity or access to difficult spiritual spaces, you can call on this tree; the oak tree is durable and strong, so if you are needing fortification or firmness, you can gain power from this tree. When respected as living, breathing beings, trees can provide insights into the workings of Nature, cycles, and our own inner essence. Each birth time is associated with a particular kind of tree, the basic qualities of which complement the nature of those born during that time. Appreciate the beauty of your affinity tree and study its nature carefully, for it has a connection with your own nature and lessons to impart.

MAHOGANY ★ Mahogany is a commercially important lumber prized for its colour, beauty and durability. Its reddish-brown colour darkens over time, and displays a reddish sheen when polished. Popular as a body wood for electric guitars, mahogany's primary magical functions are spiritual growth and guidance, and fertility. While most woods have a range of differing uses and applications, mahogany is very specialised, focusing mainly on these areas. Additionally, but perhaps not an entirely unrelated feature, is this wood's possessing of a powerful bond with the Earth element; it is particularly useful for channelling Earth energy.

Aside from fertility and growth, this wood does have some other uses: those of enhancing intuition, strengthening kinship bonds, and exploring and clarifying goals. An excellent wood for emotional and spiritual healing, mahogany can be used to provide guidance in these areas.

YOUR SACRED CELTIC CALENDAR TREES
★ ALDER OR WILLOW

ALDER ★ (18 March - 14 April)
WILLOW ★ (15 April - 12 May)

The Celts and other ancient peoples had many beliefs and traditions based around the magical lore of trees. The system of Celtic tree astrology was developed out of a natural connection with the

Druids' knowledge of Earth cycles and their reverence for the sacred knowledge they believed was held by trees. The Druids had a profound connection with trees and regarded them as vessels of infinite wisdom. Their calendar, being based on a Lunar year of thirteen months, contains a tree for each of these Lunar months, corresponding with (but not exactly) each of the twelve western astrology zodiac signs, which are based on the Solar calendar. Because there are some crossovers, I have included two possible trees for your zodiacal birth period.

ALDER ★ Often referred to as the 'King of the Waters', alder is one of the thirteen sacred trees of Celtic and European witchcraft. Associated with the period of the year surrounding the Spring Equinox, it brings a sense of healing, balance, harmony and calm. Rebirth, fertility and equilibrium are other key features.

In Welsh mythology, the alder fought in the front line of the 'Battle of the Trees', against the Underworld. When cut, its wood turns from white to red as though it is bleeding, and this red colouring can be used as a dye for sacred cloths, bags and ribbons. Growing near water, the tree has feminine associations, yet its links to war also indicate masculine powers. Therefore, the alder symbolises the balancing of the masculine and feminine.

The survival strategies of the alder tree make it an excellent pioneer species, which fits well with the Arien spirit, being an initiator and motivator. It spawns a vast quantity of seeds and grows rapidly.

Alder thrives around water, from marshlands to rivers, and the otter often makes its home in the waterside roots of the alder tree. As a hard, oily, and water-resistant wood, alder was often used to build early bridges, as well as to construct buildings, churches and cities. It is also used to make woodwind instruments, pipes and whistles.

Alder types are trailblazers. A natural born pathfinder, you're a mover and shaker with a fiery passion, charm and the ability to mix well with a broad range of characters. Dynamic and self-assured, you can see through superficialities and will not tolerate fluff or deception. Motivated by action and results, you place a high value on your time and dislike wasting it.

WILLOW ★ Willow is traditionally found on riverbanks, growing its roots in water, connecting it with the influence of the Moon. The willow symbolises regeneration as cut willows always resprout. It is a fast-growing, hardy and resilient tree, being able to withstand severe frosts. With more than 300 evolving variants, the willow is a powerful survivor and revered symbol of witchcraft and enchantment. The wood of willow is tough but elastic, and so highly flexible that it has traditionally been used for the making of baskets. In fact, it was an important resource for ancient communities, providing withies for wicker baskets - 'Witch', 'Wicca' and 'wicked' are said to be derived from the word wicker. As a water-dwelling tree, it signifies emotional balance, intuition and water-divining magic.

Willow is the tree of emotion, love, intuition and poetic inspiration. Ruled by Cerridwen, Celtic Moon goddess worshipped by the Welsh, a deeply mysterious figure, who is the keeper of the flaming cauldron of Divine wisdom, where immortal knowledge and the Fires of inspiration are formed, the willow can gently guide us towards this illumination. Because of its connection with the Lunar sphere, its powers are said to be most effective when used at night, under the Moon. Willow types are in tune with the mystical aspects of the Moon, making them highly creative, intuitive and perceptive.

ESPECIALLY FOR AUSTRALIANS
(OF ALL ZODIAC SIGNS)

If you live in Australia, here are two Australian-based magical woods, for those who prefer to source their woods closer to home and nature. Australia has a less documented history than many European civilisations, but still has no less mythology and legends swirling in its mists of time.

EUCALYPTUS ★ Eucalyptus is very plentiful and has a wonderfully intoxicating, distinctive, clean aroma which is reminiscent of the continent's vast areas of bushland, and has played an important ceremonial and medicinal role in the culture of Australian Aborigines, who have inhabited the nation for 40,000 to 50,000 years. Eucalyptus is a wood of feminine energy whose elemental association is Earth and main origin is Australia. One of the strongest healing woods known, eucalyptus wood has been used for centuries for medicinal as well as ritualistic purposes. Heady and Earthy, the energy of this wood is clean and pure. Eucalyptus is recommended for the promotion of good, robust health, and is also related to luck, especially if regarding knowledge. An excellent tool in divination, particularly when worn as a charm to invoke luck, it brings the wearer or user good fortune when used in rituals seeking positive results.

LEOPARDWOOD (or LACEWOOD) ★
Leopardwood or the Leopard Tree, so named because of its spotted wood, carries the energies of both the masculine and the feminine, Mars (Aries, Scorpio) and Venus (Taurus, Libra), and its main affinity is with the Water element (Cancer, Scorpio, Pisces). Leopardwood is a very useful tool for divination and is associated with positive luck, earning it the label 'gambler's wood'. Overall, its energy is very positive, making it an ideal wood for use in almost any ritual or spell, especially those concerning luck, magic and divination.

THE POWER OF LOVE

Each Sun sign exudes their own love and romance style. This style is an energy unique to that sign, and has the power to magnetise to that person their true, soulful match. Unhappy or unsuccessful relationships are often the result of incompatible Sun signs, personal values, goals, hopes, viewpoints or expectations. I believe everyone has a perfect soul partner (or three!) who is especially for them, and just knowing that special person or persons are out there can illuminate your life's romantic path. In this lifetime, we may not find that person or persons, but can still experience the joys and wonders of many other significant relationships which enrich and add tremendous meaning to our lives. Some partnerships are only fleeting, but the feelings they give us can last a lifetime, while others are more enduring, and the rewards they give us and lessons they teach us can last a lifetime too. Small gestures of love on a frequent basis, consistent nurturing and communication, and making the effort to understand each other, are just four ways to keep the Fires of passion and romance burning long after the initially roaring Fire has diminished into glowing embers.

Your whole natal chart would need to be examined to form an overall picture of your romantic nature, and although the Sun is a fantastic starting point, it is not the sole consideration. Regarding these other planets, in Carl Jung's studies on psychological astrology, and in traditional synastry (the comparing of two people's natal charts to determine overall compatibility), the harmonious link between the Sun in one person's chart and the Moon in the other's (usually the man's Sun and the woman's Moon) is considered the best indication for a happy and enduring relationship. More specifically, the sextile aspect, an angle of 60 degrees, appeared most frequently between the Sun of one and the Moon of the other in fulfilling relationships. Other positive planetary contacts, such as one person's Moon to another's Venus, or the Mars to the Moon (again, traditional indications of attraction and harmony) also occurred frequently.

The feminine personal planets in a male's chart (Moon and Venus), and the masculine personal planets in a female's chart (Sun and Mars) tell a lot about the inner self and how this is projected onto relationships. However helpful chart analysis is in telling a story about your relationship style and approach, it all depends not on your chart, but on what you do with the resources at your disposal, which your chart can indeed tell you a lot about. Relationships and marriages involving harmonious planetary and zodiacal energies between the two people tend to last longer because they are simply more 'flowing' and easier.

The signs in which the four personal and 'relationship' planets - the Sun, the Moon, Venus and Mars - are placed, coupled with the aspects they make with the other planets in the chart, give important clues into understanding the often unconscious drives within you that shape your relating style, tastes, mannerisms and patterns.

Expanding upon the other planetary considerations is beyond the scope of this book, but it is useful to know, particularly if you are interested in examining the dynamics of a current relationship a bit deeper, or are wishing to attract a new one into your life. But for now, your Sun sign is a wonderful place to start! Your Solar sign is regarded as being at the core of the complex - and very fun - study of relationships! So for now, we will begin this study of love with your essence, your core self, the brightest light shining from within - your Sun sign!

SOME LUCKY-IN-LOVE TIPS
GENERAL HINTS

★ To attract and retain love, the Heart chakra (an energy centre within the body) needs to be balanced and clear from blockages. The Heart chakra is located in the region of the physical heart. Its Sanskrit name is *anahata*, and its symbol is a twelve-petal green lotus flower whose centre contains a green circle and two intersecting triangles making up a six-pointed star representing balance (and also could be said to symbolise six as the number of Venus). Its element is Air and its colour is green. Balance in this chakra is expressed as unconditional love for ourselves and others. Crystals that can be used to cleanse and balance this chakra are mostly green and pink stones.

★ Pink candles (two, representing a couple, or six, representing Venus, is preferable) can be used in love spells.

★ Any 'love-attracting' wishing rituals should be done on a Friday (ruled by Venus) night around the time of the New Moon (signifying the principle of increase and growth).

★ Basil, otherwise known as witch's herb or St Joseph's wort, is said to be the most potent lover herb of all. Basil vibrates to the energy of Mars, which is all about lust and sexual energy, and it is used prolifically in all sorts of love potions and rituals throughout the world.

★ Ginger has a reputation as a potent sexual tonic and aphrodisiac *. Arousing and warm, it can increase sensual vitality, particularly in men. Being warming and spicy, its vibration aligns with Mars. Saffron is also regarded as a potent, albeit expensive, aphrodisiac!

★ Wear red and pink (associated with Mars and Venus respectively), as these colours in all their shades are said to incite passion, lust and romance. Green is also connected with the heart by virtue of its association with the Heart chakra and the planet Venus, and its links with fertility, nature, abundance of all kinds, and new growth.

★ Call upon some higher spiritual help. When working your 'love magic', some planetary influences, goddesses and gods that you can call upon are. Aphrodite, Venus and Eros/Cupid, and other lesser known deities such as Juno Lucina, Demeter, Freya, Ishtar, Circe and Hathor.

★ The planet Venus has developed a rich culture of gods and goddesses associated with her varying levels of love and passion. These include the virgin - Brighid; the fertile woman - Aphrodite, (the Greek goddess); and of course Venus (the Roman equivalent); the mother and provider - Demeter; and desirous or physical love - Eros/Cupid (Venus's son).

★ The pine tree is sacred to Adonis (Venus's lover) and is said to balance the male and female energies. Pine is cleansing and protective and, as an evergreen, symbolises life. Its cones represent fertility.

★ Cardamom is said to have aphrodisiac qualities

★ The three almost universally recognised symbols of love are the goddesses Venus and Aphrodite, and the Cupid. Venus is the patroness of flowers and vegetation, and represents the regenerative cycle of creation, as well as beauty, herbs and physical love. She can be called upon for general love wishes and rituals. The dove, roses, rings, copper, apples, rosemary and the ankh are some of her sacred symbols. Aphrodite is a Greek goddess who has the ability to brings lovers together. Her names means 'of the sea' as she is believed to have been born of the foam of the ocean. She can be called upon in ceremonies and spells for affection, love, marriage and partnership. Some of her associated symbols are the Flower of Aphrodite, swans, dolphins, frankincense and myrrh. Cupid, the cherubic winged boy with a bow and arrow, is the Roman name, and Eros is the Greek name for the same deity. The son of Venus/Aphrodite, he is an aspect that represents lustful love and desire.

★ Heartsease, another name for the wild pansy, Latin viola tricolour, was one of the most popular additives to the love potions of the ancient Romans and Greeks.

★ In centuries past, when people were more in tune with nature and its cycles, ceremonies, rituals and festivals were held on certain dates or times of year. The following are some examples, and you can reawaken their powers through craft and ceremony: February 2 is Bridhid's Day, or Bride's Day, and represents the white goddess; February 14 is Valentine's Day, traditionally the greatest and most well-known love 'celebration' of the year; March 1 is one of the festival days of Juno Lucina, the light bearer and goddess of women and marriage; the month of April is especially linked to the love goddess Aphrodite; the Summer solstice which falls on or around June 21 is an important time for reconnecting with the spirit of love, fertility and marriage; August 1 is the first of three harvest festivals in the Celtic calendar: The Harvest Festival honours Demeter, the goddess of love, as bountiful mother and faithful wife; the Festival of Lights, Diwali, in October, is sacred to Lakshmi, the Hindu goddess of happiness, love, and good fortune; the Winter solstice which falls on or around December 21, marks the turning point from long dark nights to lengthening days, and is the time of the wheel of love when virgin goddesses gave birth to their children - it is also fittingly symbolised by evergreens such as pine, ivy and holly; in Mexico, December 31, the last night of the year, is traditionally 'wishing night' and is an opportune time to make a wish for a lover in the coming year, using evergreen branches to enhance your request.

* The term 'aphrodisiac' is derived from Aphrodite, the Greek goddess of love, beauty, lust and sensuality

★ GEMSTONES ★

When it comes to calling love into your life using crystals, the general rule is that any of the pink or green stones are closely aligned with matters of the heart and can therefore help you to entice the affections you seek. Although your Sun sign has its very own special gemstones, outlined elsewhere in the book, the following stones can be used by all the signs (except for the first point, which are your own sign's feature stones), as their energies and qualities contain the power to attract and create love in all its forms, from self-love to deeper soulful connections with another, or to increase states of being which open the heart, thus enhancing your abilities to magnetise love.

★ Bloodstone, Diamond and Aquamarine ★ Using your Arien luckiest crystals is a fabulous start to working on heightening your romantic zest, and making your sensual energy more potent. Red Coral and Ruby are also useful in raising your attracting powers.

★ Rose Quartz is the ultimate love stone. It invites love into your life by helping to open your heart to receive love, and gently reminding you that you are worthy of love. Connected with the Heart chakra, it is the stone of unconditional love, enhancing all forms of it and opening up the heart. It is excellent for increasing self-worth and acceptance. The colour of rose quartz is pink, the colour of Venus, the amorous planet of desire and nurturance. Balancing and calming, it helps to heal emotional pain. Wear this stone, keep some beside your bed, or sleep with some under your pillow to remind you that love it coming your way - and that you whole*heart*edly deserve it!

★ Green Aventurine is considered the 'opportunity and luck stone'. Connected with the Heart chakra, it helps us to recognise opportunities and is said to place us exactly where we need to be for good things to transpire, as energetically it opens our mind and heart to increased perception to recognise lucky elements. It also promotes new growth, optimism, and is an overall attractor of good fortune, adventure and abundance.

★ Jade, on a spiritual level, has an affinity with the Heart chakra. It harmonises relationships, and encourages compassion and the establishment of strong bonds.

★ Emerald is reputedly a stone of constancy in love, and is said to have been brought to Earth from the planet Venus. Because it is green, it also holds deep associations with the Heart chakra.

★ Rhodochrosite can be used to attract one's soul mate. This stone, as with all the pink stones, can be used as an effective love magnet. It encourages you to appreciate yourself by teaching you that you are worthy of love, wholeness and happiness - and so opening you up to receive.

★ Malachite, Citrine, Rhodonite, Moonstone, Morganite, Beryl, Ruby, Mangano Calcite, Garnet, Red and Pink Tourmaline, Tugtupite, Rutilated Quartz, Lodestone, Peridot and Lapis Lazuli are also known for their love properties, and can be used or worn to invite romance into your life, or to bring and retain enduring love.

★ Clear Quartz can be used with any of these listed crystals to amplify their metaphysical properties.

★ Shells: Although shells are not technically a crystal, but rather a natural elemental material, they are associated with love and are sacred to Aphrodite, the Greek love goddess, and are often used in magic talismans to attract romance.

★ ESSENTIAL OILS ★

The following essential oils are known for their aphrodisiac or love-attracting properties also, and can be worn as perfumes on the skin, used in an oil burner or vaporiser, dispersed in a bath, used in spell-casting and wishing rituals, sprinkled on your pillow to imbue your dreams with inspired romantic notions, or in any other creative ways you can think of! **

★ Essential oils, flowers and herbs which contain natural pheromones or like substances, or increase pheromone levels in the body, are: Lavender, Frankincense, Jasmine, Nutmeg, Ylang Ylang, Sandalwood, Patchouli and Asian Agarwood (Oud).

★ The prime love oil, which holds universal appeal, is rose. Reputedly excellent for both the mind and body, roses are the basis of more than 95 per cent of women's fragrances, and the petals have a long tradition of uplifting the spirits and soothing the soul. *Rosa damascena* is believed to be good for attracting love, while *R. centifolia*, the French rose oil base, is regarded as an aphrodisiac. Rose is traditionally accepted as the all-encompassing universal fragrance of love, blessed with a reputation for opening up the hearts of all those who come under its spell.

★ Cedarwood oil has been used since ancient times in incense and perfumes. Its deep, woody scent helps to stimulate the Base chakra, increasing sexual passion and desire. Its sedative qualities aid relaxation and encourage openness. In herbal magic, it is also associated with spells for wealth and abundance.

★ Neroli, Geranium, Almond (as a base), Basil, Thyme, Vetiver, Gardenia, Vanilla, Rose Otto, Apple, Cardamom, Lotus, Orange, Ginger, Bergamot, Rosewood and Clary Sage are also exquisitely seductive and sensual, and can be used in any way you like to bring to you that which your heart desires. These oils, when mixed with your own pheromones and magical intentions, will naturally enhance your point of attraction!

** Always research first and use with caution.

ARIES ★ LOVE STYLE

"Like all the fiery signs, Aries is a child at heart. This sometimes means he can be childish;
at other times it means he's childlike in the most spirited, warm-hearted way."
Star Signs for Lovers, Liz Greene, Arrow Books, 1980

In her quote, Liz Greene encapsulates the Ram's trusting approach to affairs of the heart. A perpetual youth, his dynamism, enthusiasm and wonder for all things related to love, courtship and romance are characteristics that he spreads around like glitter wherever he goes. A jaded, cynical Aries doesn't exist, especially when it comes to love. Aries is incapable of going halfway and will give all of himself to the intense burning heat of the moment. But the Ram is a bit of a paradox, for although he is capable of profound thought, deep feelings and surprising tenderness, he will spontaneously run off to embark on another adventure or crusade that he deems temporarily important, leaving his partner bewildered and confused. But confusion need not reign, for the Aries is a simple, soft soul with basic needs that are easily fulfilled, and when he's finished his round of battles, he'll be back in the arms of his loved one in no time. However, don't expect meek security, soothing caresses or contentment with Aries, as they are far too excitable for that. Fidelity is not one of your stronger points. It's not that you mean to be fickle when you suddenly bound away to pastures greener; simply that you've learned all you can absorb with that person or relationship, and you must find another teacher, a fresh experience. But you can be unscrupulously faithful and your honesty will probably keep you from messing around anyway.

You are a sensitive creature and surprisingly vulnerable, but it often does not occur to you that others have feelings too. An idealist at heart, you are often seeking a storybook romance but do little to sustain it because you are so puppy dog-like and restless. Although you can be infuriatingly dizzying and impetuous at times, you still love having someone special to come home to. The Aries heart always beats fast a little faster than all the other zodiac signs, especially when your passions are stirred by a new love interest. You like to take the initiative and conquer with a blind enthusiasm, and falling in love at first sight comes as naturally to you - and occurs as often - as putting your underwear on. Dynamic, confident and exciting, you adore the thrill of the chase and are the quintessential Knight or Queen in shining armour! To Aries love affairs can sometimes be turbulent and short-lived, and marital unions may suffer from getting married in haste. Indeed, wedlock usually comes early and often more than once for you. A loyal and ardent lover, you are passionate and untainted, uncomplicated and fun, childlike and adventurous; love is either a daring adventure to you, or nothing at all. You don't use manipulation or clever mind games, as you'd prefer to get straight to the point; direct is your manner, pure and simple. Ariens are persistent and incurable romantics. Overall, you love to love, because loving is a great adventure, and you sincerely believe - and innocently hope - adventures can last a lifetime.

LUCKY IN LOVE?
ARIES COMPATIBILITY

* Please note the following is based on your Sun sign alone. For a whole and integrated approach to relationship compatibility, your whole natal chart would need to be taken into consideration. Synastry (*syn*: acting or considered together, united; *astry*: pertaining to the stars) is a branch of astrology which delves into more complex areas, and is based upon the natal charts of the two people concerned, to determine overall compatibility, potential conflicts and suitability based upon celestial influences. For the purposes of length, the below information is simplified and only refers to Sun sign connections.

Aries ★ Aries ♈ ♈

When two Rams lock horns, it can either be intensely passionate and wonderful, or a fierce battlefield and battle of wills. Either way, it will be a coupling filled with energy, vigour, excitement, adventure - and flaring tempers. Explosive love or spontaneous combustion, that is the question. Given that you are both potentially so volatile and, well, 'on fire', peace, quiet, serenity and relaxation may be difficult to achieve, but you will be loyal to each other and always defend each other. Your arch enemy - boredom - will rarely arise because you are both likely to fan the flames of desire with your constant activity and enthusiasm. However, your relationship has the very real potential of burnout unless one or both of you can curb your selfishness and forceful energy. Indeed, there may not be room for two of you in the partnership and ego clashes may be a strong feature. Neither of you will be very consistent but sparks will undoubtedly fly and there will be plenty of passion while it lasts!

Overall compatibility rating ★ 7.5 out of 10
Lucky Romance Tip ★ To attract another Aries, wear the colours red or orange, and use the crystal diamond

Aries ★ Taurus ♈ ♉

Calm and steady Taurus soothes Aries's fiery haste, but the agile and quick-minded Ram might find the Bull a bit staid, unadventurous, unmoving, boring, slow and fixed. Fire with Earth is not an easy combination and since your needs, natures and tastes are so very different, there may be difficulties unless a compromise is reached - and neither of you are good at compromising. Aries thrives on the stimulus of new enterprises or challenges, whereas Taurus prefers peace, stability and reading the stock market reviews over a mug of hot chocolate or aged whisky. Very different in nature, you two have little in common. Taurus is possessive and 'stuck', while Aries values independence, adventure and movement; Taurus is simple, sensual and seeks security, while Aries is bold, experimental and seeks novel experiences; Taurus deals with tangible and practical realities while Aries is idealistic and can't cope with the mundane details of everyday life. There is potential for the frequent locking of horns that may hinder this relationship's progress - both of you are strong-willed, but in completely different ways. Taurus finds it difficult to understand Aries's dynamic and careless nature, while the Bull's need for tranquillity, domesticity, comfort, reliability and security could drag the Ram's unstoppable character down. As well, Aries becomes irritated and impatient by the Taurean's unhurried, stay-put and obstinate attitudes, and sensible Taurus will not tolerate Aries's extravagance and carelessness with her most precious resource - money. However, the Bull could help stabilise the restless Arien spirit and the Ram could assist the Taurean to lighten up and be a bit more spontaneous. If you can learn these lessons from each other without resentment brewing, you may have a slight chance of making it work. Just expect a lot of brooding and sulky behaviour if your relationship encounters a rocky period.

Overall compatibility rating ★ 6 out of 10
Lucky Romance Tip ★ To attract a Taurus, wear the colours pink or green, and use the crystal rose quartz

Aries ★ Gemini ♈ ♊

Cheekiness, childishness and mischief reign supreme with this combination. The Ram and the Twins make a stimulating mix, and you will both talk and laugh non-stop. Ariens and Geminis are both cheerful, lively and entertaining characters. You have much in common, and this is a good combination. The depth and intensity of Arien passion may take you by surprise. Your easygoing, light-hearted ways and Aries's childlike enthusiasm spark a natural friendship and rapport. You even know how to handle the Martian's notorious temper, by making them laugh. Gemini will never hamper Aries's independence or initiative, and Aries is likely to feel inspired by Gemini's lively and friendly company. If used constructively, this is a wonderful match which will fulfil, uplift and inspire both signs. Fire and Air is an agreeable combination, and since you both generate a playful, busy atmosphere, your life together will never have a dull moment. However, the Twins are cunning, cheeky and manipulative, and the uncomplicated Arien spirit may feel irritated or perplexed by Gemini's tricky and changeable nature. But Gemini's wits will usually be a good match for the Aries's fighting spirit and dynamism, and for the most part you will find it an easy, enjoyable ride. You both enjoy variety, discovery, exploring, novelty and socialising, but Aries may find Gemini talks a bit much - Aries prefers to act on impulse and ask questions later. One thing is certain with you two: you will both give each other the space you need in the relationship. Gemini is stimulated by Aries's bold, impetuous and amusing behaviours, while Aries is bemused by Gemini's fickle, inconsistent but lovable nature and social charm. Both are inspired and childlike, and will entertain each other for hours with cartwheel competitions, pulling faces and playful affections. Neither of you will take the relationship too seriously, as you know that the most important basis for any successful relationship lies in having fun together, and sharing in the delights of light-hearted friendship.

Overall compatibility rating ★ 8.5 out of 10
Lucky Romance Tip ★ To attract a Gemini, wear the colours light blue or yellow, and use the crystal citrine.

Aries ★ Cancer * ♈ ♋

The Ram's tactless and impetuous nature may hurt or confuse the sensitive Crab. Cancer admires the Aries's dash and courage, but unless the Ram is more careful and empathetic, the Crab may very well scuttle away and hide. Aries is bold and direct, the Cancerian is more timid and private, yet your Cardinal natures can combine to make a potentially powerful coupling here; your enterprising and shrewd characters help you sniff out opportunities and develop them together with initiative. Your ruling planets, Mars and the Moon, exercise two very different energies in the relationship. The Crab may prove too emotional and clingy for the adventurous, independent and impulsive Aries, and Cancer may find Aries's careless attitudes difficult to handle, unsettling, and perhaps even hurtful to their touchy nature. Cancer is home-loving while Aries feels stifled when domestically 'caged in'; Cancer has a protective, security-seeking nature whose interests lie primarily in their homes, children and families, while Aries will happily circulate amongst anyone indiscriminately. Overall, the Ram may inadvertently upset the Crab's dedicate feelings, and the Crab will react with passive resistance through retreat or worse, sulking and bottling her emotions inside. If Aries can muster up enough patience and emotional empathy to cope with this fragile and moody character, this relationship stands a chance of working. Otherwise, over time, the Water may indeed put the Fire out.

Overall compatibility rating ★ 5.5 out of 10
Lucky Romance Tip ★ To attract a Cancerian, wear the colours silver or white, and use the crystal moonstone

Aries ★ Leo ♈ ♌

Double the dose of vitality and energy plus makes you two a dynamic duo! Fun, games and ego-trips galore will reign supreme here. Fire and Fire work well together and you find Leo entertaining, while Leo enjoys the Arien energy. Aries must beware of wounding the Leonine pride with his blunt frankness however, as this is no mere pussycat he is dealing with here. Both being Fire signs, you share bossiness, enthusiasm, courage, vibrancy, boldness and an insatiable desire for attention, praise and ego-stroking; in the case of the latter, one of you may have to move over to let the other one shine occasionally, otherwise there is a very real danger of ego clashes and the resultant tantrums. Your finer Fire qualities can be used constructively to form a wonderful bond between you, but there will inevitably be battles of wills, especially if the Ram hurts the Leo's fragile pride, in which case he will either lash out at the Aries with all paws blazing (after which he will forgive and promptly forget), or slink off somewhere to lick his wounds. Usually, he will be back for another round, as the Lion is intensely loyal and needs the support of his special other. This team has good overall prospects for happiness and fulfilment in love. You are both temperamental, warm, dramatic, vain and emotionally open - Aries just need to work on refining his flattery skills and letting his own self fall away from time to time, and the Lion will surely reward the Ram with his faithfulness and wholehearted affections. Overall, if used positively, Leo and Aries can share a joyful and stimulating relationship. And if you can make room for the two of you in the partnership, it will burn even bigger and brighter.

Overall compatibility rating ★ 8 out of 10
Lucky Romance Tip ★ To attract a Leo, wear the colours gold or orange, and use the crystal ruby

Aries ★ Virgo ♈ ♍

Virgo will find much fault with the Aries's carefree and impetuous nature, and Aries will become impatient with Virgo's nit-picking and criticism. The Ram's outspoken and direct manner puts Virgo on the defensive, even though Aries's charm and boundless energy initially intrigue the conventional Virgin. Aries and Virgo are different in almost every way, although the two of you could make a great business combination. But in love, this is a potentially difficult and challenging romance, with many clashes. Fire and Earth do not blend well together, and your partnership is a good point in case. High-speed, impulsive Aries is likely to feel frustrated by Virgo's caution, reserve, consideration of all facts before acting, and constant focus on trivial details, while the Virgin could find the Ram a bit pushy, confrontational and impetuous.

Fire is volatile and uncontrolled, whereas Earth is practical, stable and controlled, making for a great contrast in characters here. Self-restrained, aloof and cool is the Virgo, and Aries is easily put off by her rather intellectual and detached nature, however her deep sensuality and veiled charm will nonetheless intrigue him. Virgo's nit-picking and fussiness may grate on Aries's nerves, and Aries's temperamental and reckless nature will unsettle the orderly, rational and sensible Virgo. Virgo's natural tendency to anxiety and worrying will irk the live-for-the-moment Ram, and he will not understand her obsessiveness and pedantry with what he considers the petty and mundane side of life. Moreover, Aries will not understand the systematic orderliness and lack of spontaneity in the typical Virgin's character, and will either learn to live with it or, more likely, take off and not be seen for dust. If a good mental affinity and rapport can be built despite these differences, these two can make it work - but ultimately, the Aries is too footloose and fancy-free to be tied down by the Virgin's exacting and impossibly high standards.

Overall compatibility rating ★ 5 out of 10
Lucky Romance Tip ★ To attract a Virgo, wear the colours white or yellow, and use the crystal sapphire

Aries ★ Libra ♈ ♎

The loud and tactless Ram can upset Libra's delicate sensibilities. As Libra's natural opposite, Aries also wields a pull-push attraction, one moment irresistible, the next impossible. Opposites attract so you two are good friends and lovers. The Ram just shouldn't take Libra's seductive charm too seriously - it's often just a harmless game for them. Fire works well with Air, and you two have the potential to share an intense and explosive meeting of the spirits. Since these two signs are naturally friendly and need the company of others, they can share these pleasures together. However, Libra is the epitome of the personal lover, while Aries is the archetypal selfish 'me-first' lover, whose needs are paramount in the relationship. Libra's constant weighing and vacillating may irritate the Aries, and his indecisiveness may attract or repel.

If a conflict arises between you, you will stay and fight while Libra gets upset or leaves. Initially, there is often a strong attraction between you, and once it slows down to a smouldering simmer, the diplomatic Scales will usually be able to smooth any ruffled Arien feathers, making the relationship work. While Aries is largely spontaneous, blunt and frank, acting now and thinking later, Libra uses diplomacy, grace and tact to handle things. Neither will make impossible demands on the other, as both are intellectually-based rather than feeling, smothering types, but this relationship can only work if Libra allows Aries the independence he seeks and does not demand too much of him, for the Ram is childlike and as free as the wind by nature, and needs room to explore and adventure.

Overall compatibility rating ★ 8.5 out of 10
Lucky Romance Tip ★ To attract a Libran, wear the colours pink and blue, and use the crystal opal

Aries ★ Scorpio * ♈ ♏

Watch out for the clash of titans here! Being ruled by the same mighty planet Mars (albeit the secondary ruler of Scorpio), you're both such forceful and passionate characters that it can turn into warfare. You may have some memorable fights - and equally memorable 'kiss and make up' moments afterwards! Aries's passion and Fire attracts the more reticent Scorpio, but the Ram's impatience and blunt comments may insult the Scorpio's controlled but deeply sensitive nature. This is an intense combination, with the potential for explosive fireworks, aroused tempers, and a battle of the (very strong) wills. Although Water can put the Fire out, here it may serve to make it simmer, spit and spark in all directions. Scorpio is intensely emotional and naturally possessive, and this doesn't always sit too well with the more independent and less emotional Aries. Scorpio may well feel rejected and be left cold by Aries's apparent disregard for her complex feelings. If Scorpio tries to dominate the indomitable Aries, rebellion will result, and when a serious rift develops in this relationship, Aries can easily separate and cut the losses, while Scorpio may brood, sulk and harbour feelings of revenge or vindictiveness. Scorpio is passionate and controlling, while Aries will not be controlled by another, and invariably needs space.

Still, this is a particularly sexy and passionate blend of energies and both signs will relish the emotional intensity it evokes. Fire and Water creates a highly charged association to say the least, but since Mars rules over you both, you will likely share a mutual appreciation of each other's strengths and capabilities. Forthright and naïve Aries will not suspect the devious, secretive ways of the Scorpion, and whether this is a good or a bad thing is up to you to determine. Whether this will be a long-term relationship or not is very much in the balance - if you can find any! Overall, you are both strong-willed, forceful and determined, so if you can channel your combined forces into a common goal, great achievements are possible in this relationship.

Overall compatibility rating ★ 7.5 out of 10
Lucky Romance Tip ★ To attract a Scorpio, wear the colours red or burgundy, and use the crystal malachite

Aries ★ Sagittarius ♈ ♐

When two Fire signs unite, sparks can fly. Compatibility, excitement, passion and mental stimulation will keep this Fire burning. Fire and Fire blend well together, but the Sagittarian need to seek broader horizons may make Aries feel insecure and not a priority in the Archer's busy life. After all, Aries needs to be first in everything, and a priority in *everyone's* life. The Archer's lack of commitment and regard for the Ram's sensitive ego can also be points of conflict. But for the most part, this relationship has dazzling potential. Stimulating, exciting, sincere and honest are the four best words to describe the Aries-Sagittarius partnership. Sagittarius encourages enthusiastic, active Aries who appreciates the Archer's optimistic outlook and frank honesty.

Being so concerned with the self, Aries also reveres Sagittarius's broader brand of vision and deeper philosophical nature, and will be riveted by the Archer's effortless charm and intelligent wit. Both of you will allow the other freedom, adventure and space to roam, as these are so intrinsically important to you equally. You may also take many trips together, as you share a love of novelty and new horizons. The Archer and the Ram are a naïve and idealistic duo, making the chances of success together likely. Overall, you both have the faith in the journey to make it work.

Overall compatibility rating ★ 9 out of 10
Lucky Romance Tip ★ To attract a Sagittarius, wear the colour deep purple or royal blue, and use the crystal zircon

Aries ★ Capricorn ♈ ♑

This is a challenging match and likely to test your patience. When the Ram tells it 'like it is' or tries to force the pace, the gentle but strong Goat may want out. But if you two decide to cooperate, you can achieve a lot together. If Aries tries to get into competition with the Goat, the Goat may throw

Earth on the Ram's ideas and dampen his Fiery passion. Earth and Fire can be a difficult combination at the best of times, but you are both Cardinal signs, so you do share the qualities of leadership, initiative and drive. But Capricorn, an Earth sign, is traditional, sensible, practical, conventional and structured, while Aries is spontaneous, bold, buoyant and extroverted, making your natures inherently different. Aries's ruling planet Mars is impatient and fiery whereas Capricorn's ruler Saturn is sombre, cautious and deliberate.

The Goat likes to plan ahead, while the Ram prefers to push through the fence and act now. Capricorn and Aries both have highly ambitious natures, but the way they express these is completely different - Capricorn is single-minded, ruthless, and will stop at nothing to reach the top, while Aries is a big softie at heart, completely at odds with Capricorn's sometimes cool, authoritative character. Arien behaviour often undermines Capricorn's desire for stability, security and consistency. The Ram seeks out thrills, adventures, novelty and action, while the Goat is rigid, conservative, straight and respectful. However, you share an enviable competitive streak and fighting spirit of a high order, and if you can channel your energies into developing a rapport and natural respect for each other, a mutually fulfilling relationship could very well develop. Overall though, Aries's impetuous and irresponsible streak will unnerve and unsettle the quiet, steady Goat, who just wants to live a peaceful - albeit constantly striving and achieving - life. If you can both exercise tolerance for each other's differences, there is a chance your horns and your strong characters can intertwine and join forces - and you may just make it over the finish line *together*.

Overall compatibility rating ★ 6.5 out of 10
Lucky Romance Tip ★ To attract a Capricorn, wear the colours brown or black, and use the crystal garnet

Aries ★ Aquarius ♈ ♒

The interaction between your ruling planets, Mars and Uranus, and your elements, Air and Fire, ensures there will indeed be tremendous power between you two. Aquarius will never hamper Aries's independence or initiative, and Aries is likely to feel inspired by Aquarius's lively and friendly company. Aries loves anything novel, so Aquarius' offbeat character will appeal, but the hot-headed and passionate Ram is likely to become impatient and irritated with the Water Bearer's unpredictability, cool indifference and aloofness at times. When ideas flow, you are at your best together. Despite the mental affinity, that Aquarian coolness can confuse and concern Aries. Aries will also not always readily tolerate the 'embrace-all-peace-love-and-brotherhood' attitude of Aquarius, as Aries likes to always be right in the centre of the (relationship's) Universe. If used constructively, however, this is a wonderful match which will fulfil, uplift and inspire both signs.

Overall compatibility rating ★ 8 out of 10

Lucky Romance Tip ★ To attract an Aquarian, wear the colours electric blue or turquoise, and use the crystal aquamarine

Aries ★ Pisces * ♈ ♓

Aries and Pisces seem to understand each other's vulnerabilities and can develop a deep rapport. However, the Ram may find the Fish's 'poor me' attitude and tendency to daydream without taking affirmative action rather hard to take. The interaction between your ruling planets, Mars and Neptune, and your elements, Fire and Water, ensures there will indeed be a tremendous strength of romance and passion between you two. Pisces may be a little dreamy and dilly-dallying for the more active, on-the-go Arien, and Aries's sharp, direct tongue may upset the sensitive Piscean soul once too often. Pisces' tendency towards indolence and co-dependence on their partner may not sit well with the free-spirited Arien nature, which strives for independence, freedom and adventure. Being youthful at heart, however, the Ram is likely to feel inspired by the Fish's creative, unique and idealistic nature, but may lose patience when the Fish fails to deliver the goods; Aries needs immediate, snappy results, and Pisces lacks any sense of immediacy.

The hot-headed and passionate Aries may place demands upon the delicate Pisces, who may in turn swim off in the other direction; both love their freedom, but in entirely different ways. Aries likes to always be right in the centre of the Universe, and will find the Pisces readily and happily accommodates this need. If used constructively, the Water needn't put the Fire out; instead, it has the potential to produce much romantic steam. If the Ram can somehow fathom the nebulous, mysterious substance of which Pisces is made without becoming frustrated, this pairing has the potential to fulfil, uplift and inspire both signs.

Overall compatibility rating ★ 7.5 out of 10
Lucky Romance Tip ★ To attract a Pisces, wear the colours mauve or sea green, and use the crystal amethyst

* With all Fire and Water combinations (i.e. Aries with Cancer, Scorpio or Pisces), it is easy to see how and why fire and water are natural enemies. Water can quickly put a fire out, and fire can dry up water. Fire usually works quickly, and water gently. In alchemy and astrology, both are important, and both must be carefully manipulated and controlled to make full effective use of their powerful, albeit vastly differing, natures. Fire can be brought back to a steady heat, whereas the pressure and force of water can be increased vigorously or to circulate more actively. As warm and watery beings, the human body demonstrates the miracle of fire and water combined. Water connects, flows and lubricates, and brings healing, its passive, gentle nature soothing away the scorching harshness of fire. One ancient text offers a mystical view of how water and fire are intertwined in the body, and suggests that it is through consciously combining these two elements that we can transform our inner state. Fire can initiate and inspire this quest for self-transformation, but once the fire burns down, life can be restored anew by water. Natural enemies? Mostly. Astrological passion? Absolutely!

YOUR TAROT CARDS ★ FOR LUCK, MAGIC, ENERGY, ABUNDANCE, QUESTING & MEANING
THE EMPEROR, THE TOWER & JUDGEMENT

Tarot and astrology are inextricably linked. All the cards of the Major Arcana, which comprises 22 of the Tarot's 78 cards, are 'ruled by' or connected with either one of the twelve zodiac signs, the planets and luminaries, or one of the four elements.

The 22 Major Arcana cards contain the richest symbolism of all the cards in the Tarot deck, each carrying a myriad of messages for the reader to decipher. The symbolism contained within these images represents the archetypal aspects of your character. It also describes the path your soul takes through each stage of life, revealing clues through which you can explore different parts of yourself. Each of the cards also represents an aspect of universal human experience and has a name that either directly conveys the meaning of the card, such as Strength or Justice, or depicts individuals that represent these human archetypes, such as the Hermit or the Empress. The illustrations on each card contain one or more figures and tuning into a card's imagery enables you to grasp its meaning intuitively. Consider the demeanour of the characters, whether it is day or night, the background, any symbols, the buildings, the colours, the vegetation, the weather and the season. Every card has its own story to impart, and through entering that story you can gain deeper insights into the full picture of your journey so far, as well as illuminating your path ahead.

I have outlined three cards here for your sign: The Emperor, The Tower and Judgement, all of which have links to your zodiac sign itself Aries, your ruling planet Mars, and your element of Fire. All three cards will have special meaning for your sign, and can carry powerful messages and lessons for you to reflect upon.

★ THE EMPEROR ★
Ruled by Aries

Keywords ★ Discipline, Authority, Structure

★ KEY THEMES ★
Authority ★ Father ★ Boss ★ Material Wealth ★ Leadership ★ The Power to Influence ★ Organisation ★ Logic ★ Structure ★ Certainty ★ Discipline ★ Temporal Power ★ Action ★ Energy ★ Assertiveness ★ Material and Moral Power ★ Strength of Character ★ Concrete Realism ★ Objectivity ★ Willpower ★ Stoicism ★ Material Status

Number ★ 4
Astrological Signs ★ Aries & Scorpio

Just as the Empress is the feminine, the Emperor represents the masculine side of each of us, the animus. This card is about responsibility, authority, and reason, all ideas we associate with a father figure.

THE FOOL'S JOURNEY ★ The Empress is the Fool's mother, the Emperor his father. Leaving behind the natural feminine softness of his mother, the Fool comes across the Emperor, who complements the Empress absolutely by portraying the opposite characteristics. The Emperor is a mature man who is seated upon a brilliant gold carved throne adorned with the heads of eagles. The powerful eagle is a regal bird that is symbolically and literally able to fly higher than any other, with the keenest eyesight of all the birds.

The Emperor wears a gold Crown, a symbol of status and authority. While the Empress reclines comfortably on soft cushions, the Emperor sits bolt upright upon his grand throne, ready for action, conjuring up an impression of power, influence and wealth. As the Empress is the mother, so the Emperor is the father, the giver of life, the 'owner' who has sown the Divine seed. His task is to teach the Fool how to handle the material side of life, and how to live in and deal with the world of men. Instructing him on matters of authority and administration, and imparting guidelines on moral and ethical behaviours, the Emperor teaches wisdom of a worldly nature and is essential to the Fool's development. The Emperor is the dynamic symbol of drive, ambition and fame, and the channelling of energies to make ideas solid and workable. He denotes a time to take control of life in a material and concrete sense.

THE MESSAGE ★ Where the Fire of the preceding female Empress card is shamanistic, healing and sensual, the Fire of the Emperor is warlike, ascetic and domineering. In astrological terms the Magician's Fire is Arien: "I Am," while the Emperor's Fire is Leonine: "I Will." Fiery nonetheless, hence its connection with Aries, the impulsive, independent, strong-willed, bossy, authoritative leader of the zodiac.

The Emperor symbolises the intellect - creative, powerful building tool of the human mind - having detached itself from nature, the heart and the emotions, and makes it function now in an autonomous, orderly, dissociated manner. The Emperor, through his stern rulership and overseeing of others, is keen to make his ideas and plans solid and tangible. He signifies that although your dreams are valid and sound, they still need guidelines and structure so that they can manifest effectively. It therefore is important to create a detailed plan for how you wish to proceed, and maintain firm and authoritative control over how that plan is implemented; it is imperative that you cultivate logic, discipline and organisation.

When the Emperor appears in a reading, it implies you are up against a patriarchal structure of some kind, and probably have to deal with rigidity, confrontation with authority, or someone who is in a position of power over you (e.g. a boss, a father) who is egotistical, self-centred, out of touch with his feelings, and is not easy to get along with. Perhaps he represents *you*, and the realisation that perhaps your intellect has become rigid, your beliefs fixed, your creativity stunted in some way - whatever the case, maybe you just need the right outlet in order to loosen up and express your feelings with more flow. Most of all, what is needed here is a return to the consciousness represented by the Empress card - the goddess of archaic wisdom and compassionate understanding. The childlike wisdom of the Fool - the first Tarot card - can also help loosen up the Emperor's firm grip on his need to control his world. Overall, the Emperor is a powerful man who is in a strong position. As such he stands for material status and Earthly wisdom, rather than psychic or spiritual knowledge. He is influential because he has confidence in his abilities and personal power, and a great sense of self-control.

THE STORY ★ The Emperor is the archetypal male, relating to the zodiac sign Aries and its ruling planet Mars. He is the imposing and stern, but fair, father figure. He has acquired the skills and authority to play the game of life successfully. He can be dictatorial at times, may view life in a serious manner and not possess a great sense of humour, but he can be depended upon for his steadfast nature, reliable character and worldly-wise advice.

SYMBOLISM *★ The Emperor card contains imagery and symbols that represent authority and that command respect and obedience. The Emperor, a regal man of middle-age appearance, and dressed in ornate robes surveying a barren domain, governs the qualities of leadership and his role is to create stability and structure, lay down boundaries, exert power, and to make and enforce rules and laws. His rules will keep you safe and secure and his guidance is firm but fair.

Many Tarot decks show the Emperor seated on a throne carved with a Ram's head atop, signifying its link with the zodiac sign Aries. At his feet is a shield bearing the device of an imperial eagle, a symbol of worldly power and aspiration.

Only one side of his face is seen, which suggests he is only concerned with one side of life. His expression is stern and unbending, indicating high honour, unwavering ambition, control, influence, and that he takes himself seriously. His posture also indicates his focused intent; he leans to the left, holding his shield, as if he is either listening closely or is about to spring into action.

The Emperor wears the rich robes of a king and holds a royal spectre in his right hand, sometimes with another Ram's head, giving him a regal air of authority.

The Emperor's main divinatory meanings are worldly power, masculinity, potent creativity, worldly gain and achievement, confidence, stability, authority, wealth, an indomitable spirit, warrior tendencies, patriarchal figure, father, brother, husband, male influence, domination of intelligence, and reason over emotion and passion. He also indicates the desire to be a success, the making of wise choices, security, fatherhood, and the respect of others. The Emperor card signifies high honour, the achievement of ambition and it may show an influential male whose help may be required. It also represents a man in control of any given situation.

The Emperor is the certainty of life, of successful power. He has an air of power and dignity. He generally sits on a throne, holding symbols of power such as an orb and sceptre, and in some decks he carries a sword, signifying masculine potency and temporal authority. The Emperor's power is a worldly one, a strong will to impose his rules and to exercise his sovereignty over the material, concrete, tangible reality of this world. He possesses a robust character strengthened with certainties and convictions; he achieves, produces and protects. His intelligence is supreme; it is the practical and logical intelligence often seen in those in positions of power.

The Emperor represents authority figures, such as the Father, your boss, head of an organisation, or an alpha male. Don't expect fun and frolicking when this card appears, as it represents a symbol that imposes rules which must be obeyed. He is a disciplined, successful and sometimes dogmatic man, who believes only what he can see and what he can prove.

In contrast to the Empress, a symbol of maternal influence, The Emperor symbolises paternal dominance, presiding over the realms of finance, politics and material resources. While the Empress attends to the human need for emotional and physical nourishment, the Emperor strives for advancement in the wider world, employing the masculine energy required to build cities and make laws. He also indicates the kind of energy required to transform ideas into reality. However, inclined he is to act, starting things and not finishing them are key features (much like the Arien tendency to do the same!).

The Emperor is old and wise, and has himself learned that premature, impetuous action does not pay off - and warns you against it. He encourages you to be firm but not ruthless; assertive tendencies must be controlled and you must exercise patience when dealing with others. The Emperor reminds you that being in a powerful position increases the amount of responsibility you carry. Further, he encourages females to become assertive and independent.

Ariens are recommended to carry one of these cards with them to illumine their paths, and to magnetise that for which they are asking. Go forth and claim the magic which is yours by using the symbolism of the Emperor as your guide.

★ THE TOWER ★
Ruled by Mars

Keywords ★ Collapse, Upheaval, Rebuilding

★ KEY THEMES ★
★ Liberation ★ Awakening ★ Unforeseen Calamity ★ Upheaval ★ Destruction ★ Upset ★ Blessing in Disguise ★ Drastic Change ★ Relief ★ Inevitable Collapse ★ A Significant Life Event ★ Time Running Out ★ Confusion ★ Collapse and Ruin ★ A Chance to Rebuild ★ Shattering ★ Total, Inevitable but Salutary Change ★ Evolution ★ Necessary Crisis or Break ★ Catastrophe ★ Sudden Awareness

Number ★ 16
Astrological Sign ★ Aries & Scorpio

Lightning can strike without warning, and the Tower serves to remind us that sometimes change can come out of the blue. Sometimes it's change for the good, and sometimes it can be more difficult. A wonderful haiku to put the Tower into perspective is: "My barn having burned down, I can now see the Moon."

THE MESSAGE ★ The Tower is representative of destructive and cataclysmic change - an earth-shattering stroke of illumination, a powerful revelation that leads to change, and the end of a structure once thought to be secure or solid. Liberation, upheaval and relief are all connected with this card. The Tower denotes the necessary breaking down of existing forms to make way for new ones; the destruction of the old always precedes the building of the new. This card indicates the needs to find fresh ways to do things, as the old have become rigid and imprisoning.

We often live our lives as we have been conditioned to, never examining closely whether our lifestyle really suits us, until this complacency comes crashing down around us and forces us to re-consider and revaluate. The lightning that strikes the Tower on the card represents the new visions and possibilities which await us, and which will soon be brought to our attention through an upheaval or crisis. The change may be something that happens to you, an event or situation that transforms you. You may suddenly just know your marriage is over, your job is ending, the time has come for a move. You may have a sudden lucid understanding of your own destructive behaviours or addictions and the need for an immediate and radical overhaul. These insights may be momentary, like a lightning bolt, but the effects are far-reaching and enduring. If possible, open yourself right up to the power of the Tower card. The time has come to spread your wings!

THE STORY ★ A sturdy tower erected on a hill is struck by lightning and explosively blown apart. The castellated top of the tower is lifted by the blast and fire strikes deep within, flames roar from the narrow windows as two figures fall from their ruined refuge. The security afforded by this strong, old structure, has been reduced to ruin by the forces of natural law. Flames erupt and smoke fills the air, sparks and debris fall on either side; there has been a dramatic reversal of fortune. Future plans have been aborted. The Tower represents the shock that shatters your illusions, removes the rug from beneath your feet, and clears away the refuse.

A sudden catastrophe may break down all your previous conceptions about yourself. You feel as if there is no firm foundation upon which to rest your life as the veils of illusion are torn away. This forces you to face painful truths, but also liberates you from the past and provides sudden insights. The Tower tears down your world but in doing so provides a new focus. And once the storm settles, you are free! Lightning has struck, but enlightenment is sure to follow.

SYMBOLISM * ★ The Tower symbolises the rebuilding of life upon firmer foundations after it has broken down or collapsed in some way. The Tower itself is a symbol of imprisonment and limitation; it is narrow and restrictive which, on an inner level, translates to emotional restraint. Through the effects of the Tower, your illusions are shattered and your 'world' falls apart. Yet this creates space for a new, more solid foundation upon which to rebuild.

The lightning that strikes and destroys the tower symbolises the destruction of the structure and foundation upon which the falling figures have built their lives. One figure lies on the ground, while the other tumbles to join him. The lightning bolt can also signify the power of Divine justice and the impetus for change. The golden 'rain' symbolise the regenerative energy that can follow devastation. The message of this card is that, ultimately, sometimes only a shock or catastrophe can provide the wake-up call that is needed to push you from complacency into full awareness about your situation. It also symbolises a sudden flash of insight or 'lightning bolt' inner revelation that can show you a clearer way forward. The Tower is a symbol of safety; too much trust had been placed in its thick walls. It ultimately reflects the fact that nothing can stand against the will of the inevitable or the Divine.

The Tower depicts a solidly built tower that has been struck by a bolt of lightning, causing shock and disaster to its inhabitants, who are falling to the ground. The destruction of the Tower symbolises the sudden ending of something in your life, and the possibility of new and better opportunities. A crown is often shown falling from the top of the Tower, representing the danger of vanity, conceit and pride.

Its small windows suggest a self-protective element is present that can lead to a limited outlook on life.

It indicates an important and unexpected change, perhaps even a complete break from what you have built up over a sustained period of time. If you are already cautious in all areas of life, the Tower indicates that you will benefit from any clean sweep you make, allowing for a chance to rebuild once the dust has settled.

Its divinatory meanings are complete and sudden change, breaking down of old beliefs, abandonment of past relationships, severing of a friendship, changing one's opinion, unexpected events, loss of stability, bankruptcy, downfall and loss of security.

If its message is not heeded and acted upon and/or learned from, The Tower will ensure continued oppression, the following of old ways, living in a rut, entrapment in an unhappy situation, and the sustained inability to effect any worthwhile change.

★ JUDGEMENT ★
Ruled by Pluto & the Element of Fire

Keywords ★ Evaluation, Opportunities, New Directions

★ KEY THEMES ★
★ Discernment ★ Karma ★ Reaping What Has Been Sown ★ Evaluation ★ Evolution ★ Review ★ Improvement ★ Revelation ★ Renewal ★ Favourable Assessment of the Facts ★ Objectivity

★ New Directions ★ Transformation ★ Legal Situations Resolved Favourably ★ Academic and Examination Success ★ Promotion ★ Bonus ★ A Career or Life Change ★ Moving in a Different Direction ★ Rehabilitation ★ Sound Decisions Based on Good Preparation and Evaluations ★ Recovery ★ Promotion ★ Admission of Guilt ★ Good News

Number ★ 20
Astrological Signs ★ Scorpio, Aries, Leo & Sagittarius

THE FOOL'S JOURNEY ★ Archetypically, Judgement means resurrection, the rebirth that comes with spiritual awareness and awakening. Arriving at this step on his journey, the Fool understands the possibilities of transformation that can come with change. The Fool reaches for enlightenment.

THE MESSAGE ★ Sometimes called the Angel, this card has a very simple but profound meaning - a second chance. Judgement portrays an end to suffering and the beginnings of a spiritual resurrection. Through Judgement, you are being offered a dissolution of negative past patterns and a resulting spiritual rebirth, the opportunity to review past events, and to offer forgiveness or make amends. Judgement symbolises a time of judgement, when souls rise from the dead to be judged. This card depicts an angel blowing a trumpet to awaken the dead from their graves, and announcing it is Judgement Day. Bodies emerge from their coffins with arms outstretched, often casting off funeral shrouds as they make ready to embrace the new life that is offered to them by the Angel of Judgement.

There are usually three figures rising from the dead, to represent Mind, Body and Spirit, all of which must be brought forth to be judged. The dead are praying for mercy in the hope that the sins of their lifetimes will be forgiven. They now know that their misdemeanours are being exposed, and they are hoping to be allowed to move onto a higher plane of existence. On a spiritual wavelength, this card implies that one particular phase of your soul's journey is ending, and you will shortly assess what you learned and how you dealt with the passing situation, summing up your performance and its value to you.

Judgment is telling you that at this point in your life it is time to assess and evaluate yourself, and perhaps address any underlying issues which up until now may have been ignored. To do this, you need simply to become more self-aware. Judgement emphasises that in undertaking this self-examination, you should be fair on yourself and focus on your positive character traits. It is telling you that once you have done this, like the symbolic people on the card, you will be ripe and ready to move in a new direction and onto a higher, more worthwhile plane of existence! You're either near the end of a project or at a crossroads, but either way, you are on the threshold of making an important change in your life.

THE STORY ★ The Judgement card is the respected mentor, who leads the way to a fresh perspective on life and leaves you feeling elated. Its main divinatory meanings are atonement, judgement, improvement, evaluation and finally, rebirth. In the symbolism of the Tarot, Judgement is not concerned with eternal damnation or heavenly bliss based upon this 'judgement' of your life experience so far, but instead with identifying ourselves the lessons we have learned not only from our archetypal Tarot journey so far, but through our whole life from birth onward.

It is not a time for punishment and retribution, but a time of being called to account for past actions and experiences. After facing one's 'moment of truth', one can see oneself with more clarity and acceptance, and is then able to see others in the same way. This acceptance is an understanding of the human condition, human beauty, and embraces imperfections and Divine wisdom alongside each other. Our past, having been reflected upon, ensures that a positive resolution will be reinforced. With atonement and repentance, real advancement can occur. Therefore, Judgement is less about guilt and more about self-knowledge.

SYMBOLISM *★ Judgement brings you a new sense of Self. It renews and restores, and signifies that a rebirth process is taking place within the Self. A wider perspective has become available.

The angel in the card uses a trumpet, as if to call the figures from their sleepy sense of unawareness into full awakening. The cloud symbolises that this is spiritual in nature. The figures gradually rise - they are becoming released from the bonds of the past, and begin to look upwards towards an all-encompassing, broader and joyous perspective.

In some decks, the tombs are floating in a sea or river, which associates it with the notion that a river must be crossed before reaching the Promised Land. At the point of resurrection, evaluations must be made on each soul's life; therefore, this card portrays the need to reflect on life as it has been lived so far, to decide how one should proceed in the future.

This card's divinatory meanings are atonement, self-assessment, the need to repent or forgive, judgement, improvement, rebirth, rejuvenation, promotion, development, the desire for immortality, and the moment to account for the manner in which we have used our opportunities on our life's journey thus far. The Judgement card may also signify the final settlement of a matter, and a time to pay off old debts in preparation for a fresh beginning. It suggests that that which has been lying dormant will spring to life, as symbolised by the dead rising from their coffins. Judgement also indicates that the rewards for past efforts will soon finally be forthcoming.

The word 'judgement', derived from the Latin *judicem*, means 'to show or to speak what is right'. But in the context of this card, is has another meaning: discernment. As far as Judgement is concerned, discernment takes the form of distinction, recognition and separation, and all that can be accomplished. The people in the card standing beneath the figure, wearing only their nakedness, show themselves as they are, stripped of any artifice. The light within may therefore now shine forth and they no longer have any need to feel ashamed of their nudity, or to be themselves. They can discriminate between what is true or false, just or unjust. The information that has shaped their existence and made them live in hope or in fear no longer comes from external sources, but from an internal wellspring - from *themselves*.

This is a revelation. For we are all assailed by outside forces which are often unconnected with our lives, that leave us feeling powerless and depressed. With such hubbub and chaos surrounding us, it is hard to hear our inner voice (depicted as the angel on this card) and see and feel the light of our own wisdom (represented by the rays of the Sun around the angel). If we cannot hear these things, how can we detect, dissect and discern? Indeed, Judgement foretells a revelation, a renewal, an inner vision that is more accurate, more profound, more objective and real. Its presence suggests that we can no longer lie to ourselves or hide the truth from others, bringing a relief, a cure, a reconciliation, a state of trust, a relaxing of tenseness, and total receptivity. It can also reveal a vocation, a promotion, a recognition or a reward that comes about as a result of our newfound inner consultations.

The Judgement card indicates that the time is ripe for a period of self-appraisal, which involves taking an honest look at yourself, your motivations and your actions. This means reviewing your accomplishments so far, neither under- or overvaluing them. It also advises that one should carefully consider how present actions affect others around them.

Ultimately, Judgement suggests that it is time to review, assess, evaluate and make some considered and thoughtful judgements regarding your life, and then make empowered decisions. To put it another way, in the words of Henry David Thoreau: "Go confidently in the direction of your dreams. Live the life you have imagined." It is time to practice discernment and then move in a new direction, from that newfound, redeemed, freed spirit.

* Please note that the images described are not found in all Tarot decks. The images in different decks can differ considerably.

THE TAROT'S SUIT OF WANDS ★ REPRESENTING THE FIRE ELEMENT

The Tarot Wands (known in some old decks as Rods, Staves or Batons) are connected with growth, creativity, enterprise, ambition, progress, initiative, work/labour, action, adventure, energy, vitality, willpower, reputation, fame, efficiency, achievement, challenge and all creative matters. The Wands represent the Fire element, and their Fire is mainly influenced by the planet Mars, which activates travel and work energy, and sexual force, but they also partake the energies of Jupiter - the Fire of benevolent warmth and expansion - and incorporate the Fire of the Sun, radiating confidence and wellbeing in all directions.

Being of the Fire realm, the Wands are also associated with dynamic action, inspiration, passion and determination. Like fire itself, they signify the ignition and generation of warmth and energy, while also burning off the dross and impurities of life. Fire creates light and heat, but it can too readily burn and easily rage out of control, which can lead to destruction, ruin and havoc. However, the energy of fire can also be transformative. It needs fuel in order to be effective, and if this vital fuel is sourced only from the feelings, flames can be swiftly burned out. Therefore, the ultimate source of fuel for this brand of fire lies within the self's sense of connection with the spirit - as this is a deep well that never runs dry.

The narrative of the fiery Suit of Wands propels you forward and defines your actions and motivations in life. It tells of the need to create change and movement, always beginning with the initial spark that sets the flames of passion ablaze. If Wands predominate in a reading, there's a high chance you are actively engaged in accomplishing your goals. They deal with the physical and spiritual life force - positive conflict, struggle and passion all being part of its expression. They reveal how active, dynamic, enthusiastic and passionate we are, and how these are experienced and expressed by us. There are often elements of struggle with the Wands suit, because energy needs to move freely and spontaneously, and any blockages to this have to be shifted. Conflicts within the Wands cards are generally not considered serious, and lead to a deeper, more profound sense of Self once they are resolved.

They also govern inspiration and the spark that can appear out of the blue to light the way forward. In a deck of playing cards, the Wands correspond to the suit of Clubs.

THE LUCKY 13 ★ ARIEN TIPS FOR INCREASED MAGIC, LUCK & MAGNETISM

1 ★ Incorporate Arien symbols into your daily life to remind yourself of your soul's mission.

2 ★ Use the precious gem Diamond in any form in your daily life - wear it, meditate with it, hold it and carry it with you everywhere! Diamond is the stone of love and endurance. It also brings fortitude, clarity, enlightenment and spiritual evolution. As a universal symbol of wealth, it might even attract material riches if that is what you are seeking. Above all, it is a solidified tonic which helps to strengthen bonds of all kinds, and attract wonderful things to you.

3 ★ Wear or surround yourself with the colours red, orange and other bright autumnal shades.

4 ★ Learn the way of the Scales, your opposite sign, by learning the arts of balance, moderation, tact, calmness, grace, diplomacy and consideration of others. Libra has much to teach the Aries soul. Come gently into your centre … Learn the ways of elegance and subtlety … Focus on others rather than the self … Feel the joy of give-and-take relationships … Consider all choices before acting … Celebrate your relationships and what you contribute to them … it's *all* within you!

5 ★ Use your lucky numbers 7 and 9 whenever you are needing an extra stroke of luck.

6 ★ Magnify and celebrate your sense of self, your innate confidence, your ability to inspire and uplift, your childlike sense of wonder and enthusiasm, your inborn joy, your inherent generosity of spirit, and your loyalty to those you love.

7 ★ Remind yourself of your quest constantly, that is by speaking, breathing and *truly living* your personal dreams and insights - and share them with others who can help make them come true!

8 ★ Focus your energies on developing more balance and self-reflection in your life. Connect with what you can give to relationships rather than simply what you can take. Tap into your ability to share and receive through any means possible - yes, it is in there!

9 ★ Use your innate powers of boldness, courage, boundless energy, awareness, pure belief and eager metaphysical attunement to visualise and draw that which you desire towards you. If you can develop simple faith in the positive outcome of events, you can easily use your inexhaustible enthusiasm to great creative effect.

10 ★ Tap into and utilise your ability to lead, inspire, guide, and transform others through sharing your emotions, spirit and soul. But to do that, you'll need to temper your impetuosity and headstrong need to always win. Sometimes coming second or third can be just as glorious. Allow someone else to step up to the podium from time to time.

11 ★ View your vast stores of energy and vitality as strengths and call forth the powers of your robust sense of self. Be who you *really* are, without reservation or apology, and the rest will fall into place.

12 ★ Become the 'Leading Enlightener' of others - and yourself - that you were born to be! Selfishness has no place in the true race to the top - there's room enough for others up there too! And as Scorpio Zig Ziglar so rightly proclaimed, "Remember, there is plenty of room at the top."

13 ★ Once you have mastered grace, diplomacy and tact, as well as a greater focus on others, learn to share the resulting abundance, insights and knowledge with other people so they too can walk the Higher Path!

HAVE YOU PACKED YOUR MAGICAL BAG FOR THE JOURNEY?

If you wish to increase and draw more luck, love and abundance into your life, a power pack is essential. For Ariens, I would recommend carrying or wearing the following items on you on your travels. Then just sit back and watch as magic pours into your experiences and realities, both inner and outer!

★ One of each of the following gemstones: Bloodstone, Diamond, Aquamarine, Ruby
★ Tarot cards The Emperor and The Tower (and Judgement too, if you wish)
★ A hawk in any form (use your imagination!)
★ Something made of iron
★ An axe symbol in any form
★ A postcard or image from a hot, dry place (representing your Choleric disposition). Bon Voyage!
★ A postcard from the future to yourself, proclaiming, 'Wish You Were Here!'

A FINAL WORD ★ TAPPING INTO THE MAGIC OF ARIES

There is something inherently magical about Aries, the hot-headed Ram. Nothing is tentative about you. The cosmos has endowed you with the precious and important gifts of decisiveness, strength of conviction, bravery, heroism, passion and a complete lack of pretension. Whether you are fully cognisant of it or not, a magical reservoir of energy is available to you to tap into whenever it is needed.

Blessed with an inexhaustible storehouse of optimism, get-up, hope and wonder, you truly are the uplifting star of the zodiac, affecting everyone around you with your powerful and infectious cheerfulness. Never malicious but ever self-serving and confident, the Arien soul yearns to connect with life's fun and feisty side. To really tap into your true magic, this connection with fun is imperative to your life's spring of wellbeing. Inside anyone who has a strong Aries influence in their natal chart, is a person who appears to think that he is more interesting and important than others and better than those with whom they are in competition, but deep down the Aries seeks approval and belonging. This manifests as an almost single-minded aim to win at all costs, but even having won, the secret Aries still fears they will not be liked or valued. Most Ariens are not as confident as they appear; fears can sometimes overcome them but they will never reach the surface, for they are fiercely protective of their robust egos, and their inner warrior will always ultimately triumph over any fears or insecurities.

Finally, to attune yourself to luck, harmony and success, Ariens should wear, eat, inhale, meditate upon, create, design, and dance with any or all of the suggested luck-enhancers for your Sun sign to receive the most beneficial astral vibrations these 'boosters' can offer you. Wearing, decorating and working with the amazing powers of all your lucky guides, animals, crystals, colours, woods, cards, herbs, foods, places, talismans, planetary influences, charms, numbers, and other magical tips contained within the words of this very book, will bring you greater abundance, love, magic, energy, happiness and personal power, and attract all manner of things to you like bees to sweet flowers. This, my Arien friends, I promise you - and Aquarians *never* lie.

Good luck on the rest of your amazing life journey, and may LUCK always smile upon you!

Lani is also available for personal Astrology, Numerology, Aura * & Tarot reading consultations, via post, email, Skype and in-person.

Please email lalana76@bigpond.com for more information.

In-person only

Facebook Page ★ Astrology Magic

Other Books in the **Lucky Astrology** Series

Lucky Astrology ★ Taurus
Lucky Astrology ★ Gemini
Lucky Astrology ★ Cancer
Lucky Astrology ★ Leo
Lucky Astrology ★ Virgo
Lucky Astrology ★ Libra
Lucky Astrology ★ Scorpio
Lucky Astrology ★ Sagittarius
Lucky Astrology ★ Capricorn
Lucky Astrology ★ Aquarius
Lucky Astrology ★ Pisces

Order your copies now, from White Light Publishing House, at www.whitelightpublishingau.com

www.ingramcontent.com/pod-product-compliance
Lightning Source LLC
Chambersburg PA
CBHW071157300426
44113CB00009B/1230